I0102584

69 Ways to Make Love...

...without having sex!

Traci Peraza-Williams

69 WAYS TO MAKE LOVE WITHOUT HAVING SEX
Copyright © 2021 by Traci Peraza-Williams

All rights reserved. Printed in the United States of America. No part of this book may be used or reproduced in any manner whatsoever without written permission from the author, except in the case of brief quotations embodied in critical articles or reviews.

Revised and Edited by Angie Antoine
Cover Art and Interior Illustrations by Axel Olson

ISBN-13: 978-1-7352030-1-0

First Edition: September 2021

Contents

Preface

I was inspired to write this book during a conversation with a beloved childhood friend of mine. He was expressing how much he wanted to establish a loving connection with his partner that was based on lasting intimacy, rather than just trying to cement the relationship through sex. That conversation made me realize how much I needed to share this truth today: everyone feels so free to experiment sexually, yet they also feel frustrated when they can't experience real intimacy and true love. Sexual intercourse is rarely, if ever, the glue that binds lasting relationships, nor is it the main component that makes a truly loving relationship satisfying and fulfilling.

My hope is to provide lovers with opportunities to engage in activities that encourage them to demonstrate tenderness, thoughtfulness, openness, and vulnerability, discovering what it means to truly satisfy one another. While this book includes racy, sensual, and provocative ideas for lovers to explore, the goal is to help couples create moments that build lasting bonds.

I truly believe that any couple who devotes their hearts to exploring and improving these 69 activities within 12 months will fall into deeper love than before—come on, I dare you!

Some of you might already have experience with a few of these activities, so you and your partner may already know what to do. If this is the case, then I challenge you to use the ideas I provide to improve the way you experience those activities together.

Set the stage. Thoroughly plan and prepare for a romantic rendezvous each and every time. Prepare the kinds of beverages, foods, music, and atmosphere conducive to romance.

Establish the tone. Know what you and your partner are expecting to achieve from a given activity and do whatever needs to be done to make sure your bond is strengthened in the process.

Monitor the mood. It's both you and your partner's jobs to make sure that you both feel safe, secure, confident, and pleased throughout every activity. Some of them may pull you and/or your partner out of your comfort zones, so try to figure out how to get the most out of every experience. The focus is not on the activity themselves: they are merely a means for you and your partner to spend quality time with each other, to affirm one another, and for you both to openly show that you cherish each other. My ultimate hope is that you build such strong bonds through these experiences that your mind, body, and soul are full! Please share your feedback—it may nudge me to do a Part 2 with more activities.

Now, go have fun—go make some love!

- Traci

Activity No. 1: The Bathing Ritual

Run a tub full of healing herbal essence, fragrant flower petals, and essential oils to infuse the water. Sprigs of rosemary, juniper, lavender, lemongrass, sage, and mint are just a few inviting herbs that arouse the senses and send warm notes wafting through the air. A few handfuls of bruised or crushed petals releasing their fragrant oils can simply be breathtaking. Those lovely red roses; those delicate purple geraniums; those sweet-scented Lily of the Valley bells; those hearty blooms of red, orange, blue, violet, white, and pink hyacinths; those lush and beautifully rich gardenias; and those lilac lilacs are all worthy of making your tub a beautiful and aromatic floating garden. If you have missed an occasion to present your lover with flowers or perfume, this bathing ritual will make up for every one of them. Just verify that neither of you have any allergies to the herbs and flowers that you use!

Make sure that your love elixir is teeming with thick ribbons of luscious, velvety bubbles. Keeping the room heated will ensure that your partner is enveloped in all the warmth necessary for maximum comfort. Set aside pots of piping hot herbal tea with a sprinkle of Ceylon cinnamon, a twist of Meyer's lemon, a sprig of Madagascan vanilla, a touch of freshly shaved ginger, or whatever else is to your and your lover's liking. Have fluffy, oversized drying towels, warmed body oil, and luxurious thick terry cloth robes ready and waiting for you both once you finish.

After you and your partner have determined which positions will be the most comfortable for both of you to enjoy, you should welcome your partner into the carefully and lovingly cultivated "water garden."

It is best if you sit at the rear of the tub furthest from the spout and guide your partner to slide into the warmth between your thighs, nestling their back against your chest. This will offer a neck waiting for the kisses you will render, ears listening for the loving affirmations you will whisper, shoulders yielding under the strength of your loving strokes, muscles relaxing from head to toe because of your tender caresses, thighs softening from the much-needed massage provided by your fingers moving rhythmically up and down, round and around.

Maybe it's time to switch positions. It might be more comfortable to sit side by side with your knees bent but hands-free to explore one another. Perhaps, it is more comfortable to just let your legs dangle casually outside the tub as the two of you sit side by side, sipping tea and enjoying all of the sensory treats.

It may be the perfect time to make a specially created playlist of some of your favorite romantic songs. A good soundtrack only helps to set the mood all the more. Hopefully, you have considered adding a few new artists and genres that you and/or your lover have never listened to before, but are sure to find enjoyable. You may want to listen to an inspiring TEDTalk, an interesting podcast, a local spoken word artist, an enlightening sermon, or just some beautiful nature soundscapes. The purpose of this time is to express all of the deep, loving, affirming, nurturing, and tender feelings that you have for one another without reservation, and without sexual intercourse being the aim. This time should be memorable—do it as often as you can! Make sure that you have planted no less than 100 kisses during this ritual!

Be as meticulous with the final details as you were with setting the stage. Step out first and leave your partner in the warmth of the bath. Bring the luxurious robe that you had selected earlier to your lover and allow them to nestle into it as it wicks away the moisture. You can also massage fragrant essential oils onto your partner's body before leaving the bathroom; make sure that these oils are safe for each and every body part. This gesture may require that your partner stands as you carefully work from head to toe. You may find parts of your partner's body more accessible to your handiwork if you kneel before them. Kneeling is also a sign of submission, gentle stroking a sign of adoration, tenderly kissing a sign of cherishing, and simply staring into your partner's eyes a sign of affirmation.

You may opt to finish the oil bath on your bed, so be sure to cover the bed in a soft bath towel or a luxurious velour blanket that won't be damaged from the lavish use of oils. Prepare the room with flower petals, fragrant candles, and romantic music. If you decide to finish with a massage, then start at the scalp and work your way down, ever so slowly, ever so carefully. It is perfectly acceptable to massage the oil into the intimate parts as well, but be fair! The goal is not to stimulate or arouse your partner sexually, but to demonstrate your affection, your adoration, and your devotion.

Planning Notes:

Who can provide "expert" knowledge, if necessary?

_____

_____

What items do you need to bring?

_____

_____

Where will the activity take place?

_____

_____

When will the activity take place?

_____

_____

Additional Pre-activity Notes:

_____

_____

Post-Activity Notes, Ideas, & Suggestions:

_____

_____

_____

_____

_____

_____

_____

_____

_____

_____

_____

_____

Activity No. 2: The Shower Ritual

This is an ideal time for partners to have a full-body exploration, because a bathtub may be too confining if one of you are too tall or not able to maintain a comfortable position in it.

Start off by placing a sachet of herbs on the showerhead to release sweet, mood-setting aromas. Fill the bathroom with fragrant candles and/or an aromatherapy diffuser. You can fill the sink with fragrant flower petals and floating aromatic candles for an added romantic touch. Since the focus of this ritual is to bathe your partner and have your partner do the same for you, have an assortment of bathing tools that provide different sensations.

These tools can include: a soft sponge that easily holds and releases sudsy concoctions; a hard bristle brush that, when wet and "driven" over dry skin, is both exhilarating and improves the circulation; a soft bristle brush that sends warmth through the body; a loofah that helps slough dead skin cells; a massaging ball or other massaging apparatus that helps relieve tension in the body; a soft towel for cleaning all the intimate body parts; and of course, loving, lathered hands that must touch every part of the body, from the head to the soles of the feet.

Keep in mind that you'll need to have body washes with the proper ph balance for intimate areas. I suggest using organic baby wash, so that you can wash your partner from head to toe without the worry of adverse reactions, including the discomfort from having soap in your bae's eyes. Use some of the same suggestions for the bathing ritual that would be applicable for creating a spectacular shower ritual!

Planning Notes:

Who can provide "expert" knowledge, if necessary?

_____

_____

What items do you need to bring?

_____

_____

Where will the activity take place?

_____

_____

When will the activity take place?

_____

_____

Additional Pre-activity Notes:

_____

_____

Post-Activity Notes, Ideas, & Suggestions:

_____

_____

_____

_____

_____

_____

_____

_____

_____

_____

_____

_____

Voglio baciarti al chiaro
di luna...

Activity No. 3: Hair Washing Ritual

This ritual is such a simple and easy way to show love to your partner. It can be added in with any of your "water love" activities.

You can set an entire mood by decorating the area with aromatherapy candles, flower petals, floral bouquets, sweet treats, inviting cocktails, bubbly, or other delicious drinks. You can also prepare to wash your partner's entire body while focusing mostly on their hair, or you can just wash their hair without washing the rest of their body. Determine the hair grooming tools that you'll need: a special comb, a detangling brush, a blow dryer, etc. Just don't guess! Either observe your lover's ritual beforehand or ask what you'll need ahead of time so that you can prepare properly.

The key is to give proper attention to scalp stimulation. A shampooing followed by an oil massage with essential oils like peppermint can be so invigorating and nourishing. A hot oil or deep conditioning treatment with a heating cap can be wonderfully relaxing as well. It's also a great time to have your partner sit and relax; while their scalp and hair are being treated, you can prepare a nice foot soak and finish it off with a nice foot and leg massage.

Other hair rituals can be added to this special time. Perhaps you can add a simple hair brushing, hair braiding, comb through, or styling as an extra treat.

Planning Notes:

Who can provide "expert" knowledge, if necessary?

_____

_____

What items do you need to bring?

_____

_____

Where will the activity take place?

_____

_____

When will the activity take place?

_____

_____

Additional Pre-activity Notes:

_____

_____

Post-Activity Notes, Ideas, & Suggestions:

_____

_____

_____

_____

_____

_____

_____

_____

_____

_____

_____

_____

_____

Activity No. 4: Intimate Apparel Shopping

This is such a fun experience, and you can do it either out on the town or from the comfort of your home, all cuddled up together on the couch. Wherever you choose, just remember that the key is to make it an experience.

If you are shopping in the town, try to find some special intimate apparel shops to explore in your area. While you are out, make it a point to grab breakfast, lunch, or dinner at a cozy romantic spot! After you've made your purchases, you can always come home, enjoy a mini bath ritual, and do a fashion show for one another.

If you are shopping online, then there are numerous options to explore. Set the mood by preparing delightful finger foods, delicious snacks, and tasty treats. Top it off with a nice bottle of wine or handcrafted specialty cocktails that you two can make together. Once your purchases are delivered, you can plan a bath, shower, hair washing ritual, or a fashion show, and make it lovefest!

Before trying on any of these garments, be sure to pre-wash each one in intimate wash. Once they are cleaned, you can help each other try on each piece and model the garments for one another. Feel free to examine the details and texture of the lingerie and underwear. Touch the silkiness and softness of the garments on your partner—feel with your hands, your feet, your face, your lips.

Experience how the garments taste on your partner's skin and their private areas, and encourage your partner to do the same with you. Discuss your favorites with each other. Do you like silks, satins, velours, laces, mesh, lycra, leather, nude, punk, fancy, athletic? Do you like more or less revealing? Remember each other's favorites, so that you can make future purchases that will please your partner.

Some of the best brands for women are as follows: Agent Provocateur, La Perla, Natori, Cosabella, Maison Close, Kiki De Montparnasse, Yasmine Eslami, Wolford, Maison Lejaby, Coco de Mer, and Simone Perele.

Some great options for men are the following: Versace, Tom Ford, Zimmerli, SKVI, and *www.mensunderwearstore.com*.

Planning Notes:

Who can provide "expert" knowledge, if necessary?

_____

_____

What items do you need to bring?

_____

_____

Where will the activity take place?

_____

_____

When will the activity take place?

_____

_____

Additional Pre-activity Notes:

_____

_____

Post-Activity Notes, Ideas, & Suggestions:

_____

_____

_____

_____

_____

_____

_____

_____

_____

_____

_____

_____

_____

진심으로 사랑해

Activity No. 5: Skinny Dip

All around the world, there are mystical, magical, and wildly romantic bodies of water where you can "make love." Whether you find your retreat on a remote private beach in the Caribbean, a crystal-clear lagoon nestled in the lushness of the rainforest, a hidden hot water spring in a little country town, a private pool in your own backyard, or a little natural pool in some cool far-off getaway, you should know that there is a wonderful place created just for you and your love.

If you can't get away and don't have a pool of your own, don't despair! You can purchase a blow-up pool and discover your inner child with your partner, right in your own backyard. Once you find your momentary paradise, do a little extra to make it a memory that can last a lifetime. Get packed for a skinny dip passion party for two. If you are daytime dipping, pack a picnic basket of fresh fruit, fresh frozen fruit smoothies that taste perfect when thawed, and finger foods that you both enjoy. If time and talent permit, create some homemade treats! Add a bottle of bubbly, a freshly-cut flower bouquet, aromatic body massage oil, organic bug repellent made from essential oils, freshly-laundered fluffy beach towels that have been scented with an aromatic laundry spray, an aromatherapy candle, and your favorite music! If you are doing a nighttime dip, make the appropriate switch-ups for your treats. Charcuterie boards, desserts, vegetable trays, dips, salads, and tasty *hor d'oeuvres* are all delightful options. Pack a flashlight and two robes, just in case you decide to take a stroll.

Whether day or night, take water toys, floats, board games, and most of all—take safety precautions. It is okay to be nude and wearing only a safety vest! Focus on enjoying one another's presence. Explore, study, and bask in each other's beauty. Give one other a massage. You could go snorkeling, or you may simply choose to wade, float, or play water sports. Keep in mind that "skinny dipping" may be illegal in some areas. Be safe and abide by the law!

According to Travel and Leisure, some of the most remote, yet beautiful beaches in the U.S., are as follows: Second Beach in Washington, Dry Tortugas in Florida, Assateague Island in Maryland, Pa'ako Cove and Kauapea in Hawaii, South Manitou Island in Michigan, Carova Beach in North Carolina, Orient Beach State Park in New York, Enderts Beach in California, Rogue Bluffs in Maine, and Cumberland Island in Georgia. Town and Country shares a list that comprises some of the most beautiful and private beaches where lovers can explore one another on the international front: Whitehaven in Australia, Englishman's Bay in Trinidad, Luskentyre in Scotland, Playa Jeremi in Curaçao, Gtyfoneri in Greece, Columbier in St. Barth's, Sunrise Beach in Thailand, Monsul in Spain, Li Cossi In Italy, and Porto Santo in Portugal.

In addition to wonderful beaches, there are picturesque falls, lagoons, and swimming holes just waiting for adventurous lovers. The site *Trips to Discover* shares an incredible list: Havasu Falls in Havasupai Indian Reservation, Tinago Falls in the Philippines, Jellyfish Lake in Palau, God's Bath in California, Makapipi Falls in Maui, Sliding Rock in North Carolina, Ik Kil Cenote in the Yucatán, Gura Portitei in Românâ, Jean Larose Waterfall in Quebec, To-Sua Ocean Trench in Samoa, Enfield Falls in Ithaca, NY, Helena Bay in Néw Zealand Petit St. Vincent in the Grenadines, and Kuang Si Falls in Laos.

Planning Notes:

Who can provide "expert" knowledge, if necessary?

_____

_____

What items do you need to bring?

_____

_____

Where will the activity take place?

_____

_____

When will the activity take place?

_____

_____

Additional Pre-activity Notes:

_____

_____

Post-Activity Notes, Ideas, & Suggestions:

Activity No. 6: Head Job

It is so important to understand the psyche, mental make-up, and personality of your partner. One of the most intriguing ways that we can open our hearts to our partners is to let them in our "head." To get started, try taking a few credible personality tests that will help in identifying and clarifying who you are and how you both show up. Spend a day taking several tests online together, sign up for a workshop given by a credible clinician, or read a related book together.

To have a truly satisfying relationship with your partner, you have to be vulnerable, transparent, and authentically you—flaws and all. Check out the following sites for tests:

- *www.myersbriggs.org*
- *www.discproflle.com*
- *www.openpsychometrics.org*
- *www.hexaco.org*
- *www.acer.edu.au*
- *www.iluguru.ee*

Planning Notes:

Who can provide "expert" knowledge, if necessary?

_____

_____

What items do you need to bring?

_____

_____

Where will the activity take place?

_____

_____

When will the activity take place?

_____

_____

Additional Pre-activity Notes:

_____

_____

Post–Activity Notes, Ideas, & Suggestions:

Activity No. 7: Chocolate Tryst

For centuries, chocolate has been the delicacy of lovers' delight, and it is one of the most frequently purchased gifts for Valentine's Day. Why not "make love" while letting chocolate take center stage? Plan a wonderful evening making chocolate with your partner!

First, order chocolate molds, but don't just order the typical molds: order naughty molds. You can order "adult" candy molds online from *www.streichs.com* or *www.nationalcakesupply.com*. There are a host of options for lovers! Go online and explore before placing your order.

There are so many melt-and-pour recipes online that will make the chocolate crafting process simple. You can purchase the ingredients from your local grocery store or online from one of my favorite stores, *www.nuts.com*. Make sure that you buy the best ingredients available for your budget.

Once you've received all of your supplies, plan your tryst. Keep it simple and fun. Make a sandwich and salad bar for you and your partner. Purchase a few bottles of wine that can be paired perfectly with chocolate. Download two of the most romantic chocolate-themed movies: Chocolat and Water for Chocolate. Enjoy the movies, while holding, caressing, and kissing your partner as your candies cool.

Once your chocolate treats have cooled enough to be enjoyed, role-play with your partner as you savor the chocolate naughty parts. Slowly lick, nibble, suck, and savor the candy body part replicas and convince your partner of how you will one day do the same to your lover's body.

Encourage your partner to role-play and demonstrate the same for you. You may also enjoy finger painting one another's bodies with warmed chocolate and clean the chocolate off one another with kisses, licks, and nibbles.

Now that you are all both sticky sweet, consider cleaning up with a refreshing shower ritual. If you have extra time, consider planning a bathing ritual to finish off the tryst!

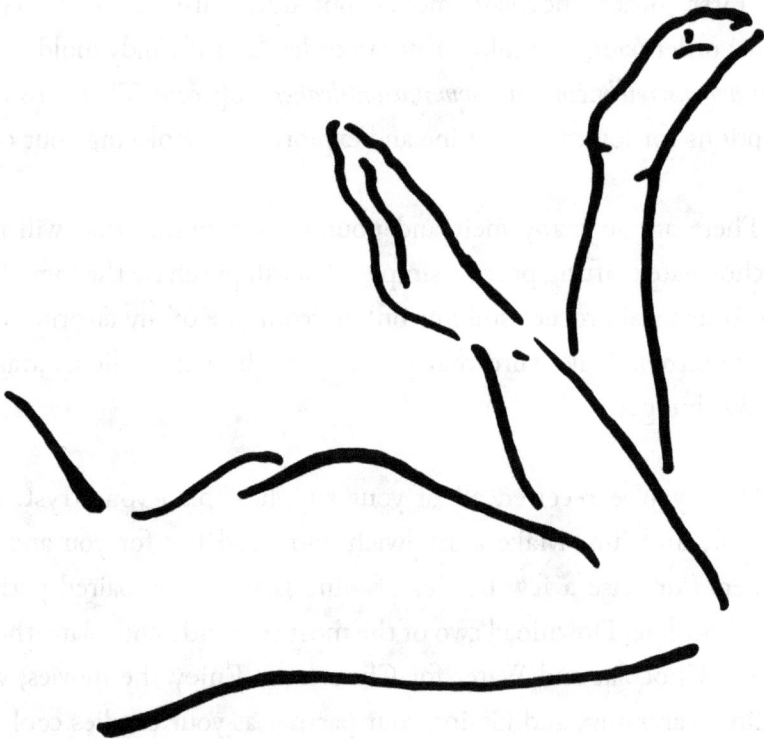

Planning Notes:

Who can provide "expert" knowledge, if necessary?

_____

_____

What items do you need to bring?

_____

_____

Where will the activity take place?

_____

_____

When will the activity take place?

_____

_____

Additional Pre-activity Notes:

_____

_____

Post-Activity Notes, Ideas, & Suggestions:

_____

_____

_____

_____

_____

_____

_____

_____

_____

_____

_____

_____

_____

Activity No. 8: A Few of Our Favorite Things

It always surprises me how much so many couples love one another, yet they often know so little about their partner or about their favorite things. It is so affirming when someone you love shows interest in what matters to you. It certainly is a fool-proof method to building unbreakable bonds. Take the time to spend an entire day discovering and uncovering a few of your partner's favorite things. I encourage you to find out how and why your partner's choices became favorites. Oftentimes, our favorites become favorites because of fond moments and memories.

Here are some of my favorites that you both can explore and experience together. Expand on this list. Enjoy!

Find out each other's favorite...
...food
...flavors
...beverage
...color
...dessert
...candy
...song
...movie
...book
...actor
...actress

...singer

...band

...car

...game

...era

...city

...activity

...day of the week

...and anything else you can think of!

Add all the favorites that you and your partner can! Keep track by making a list and update it as you move and change through your life together.

"The And" Game

This game allows you and your partner to ask one another 199 questions that you and your sweet thang probably are dying to know. These questions were taken from an Emmy Award-winning documentary that had the purpose of helping couples deepen their connection. Always take care to set the mood—bring drinks, sweet treats, finger foods, candles.

Planning Notes:

Who can provide "expert" knowledge, if necessary?

_____

_____

What items do you need to bring?

_____

_____

Where will the activity take place?

_____

_____

When will the activity take place?

_____

_____

Additional Pre-activity Notes:

_____

_____

Post-Activity Notes, Ideas, & Suggestions:

Activity No. 9: Book "Club"

Create your own book club by picking a few books for your partner and having your partner pick a few for you. You can choose books from the self-help, inspirational, religious, autobiographical, instructional, romantic, financial, art, collectible, fictional, travel, historical, or cultural categories. It's a great idea to choose books that will help you increase your understanding of and bond with one another.

You can choose books that gently help your partner understand your feelings, sentiments, or desires that may be difficult, challenging, or uncomfortable for you to express. If you want to read the same book at the same time, then you can read it in tandem and create scheduled reading dates where the two of you come together at certain times to read and discuss. If your schedules don't allow that, then you can read separately, then come together to discuss your reflections.

Whichever way that you choose to do this activity, try to make sure that you are both learning new things about each other and growing closer as a couple.

Planning Notes:

Who can provide "expert" knowledge, if necessary?

_____

_____

What items do you need to bring?

_____

_____

Where will the activity take place?

_____

_____

When will the activity take place?

_____

_____

Additional Pre-activity Notes:

_____

_____

Post-Activity Notes, Ideas, & Suggestions:

_____

_____

_____

_____

_____

_____

_____

_____

_____

_____

_____

_____

_____

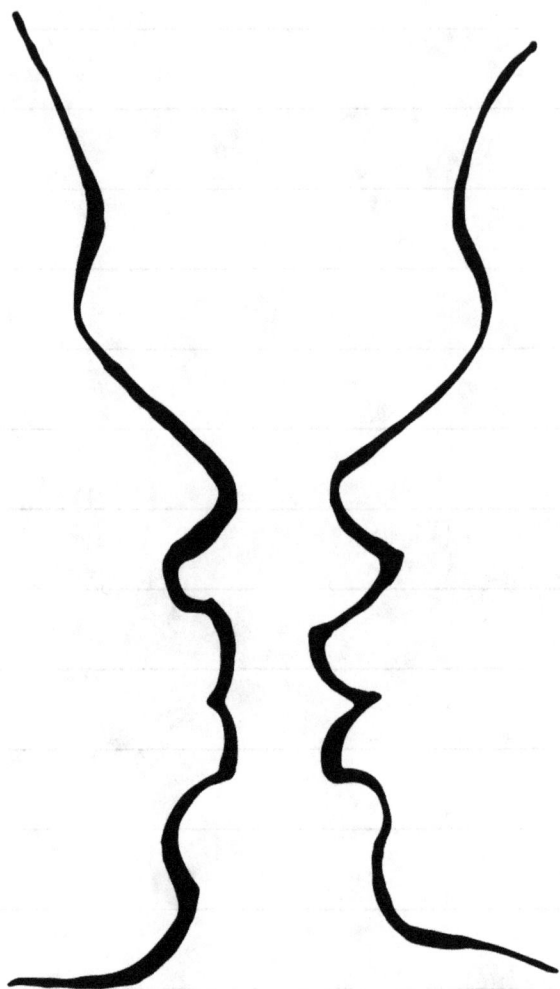

Hakuna anayemshinda
mwanaume kama mwanamke...

Activity No. 10: Never "Bored" Games

There is always a day when staying indoors is the preferred or even the best option. You may have completed all your chores, made all your "calls," and simply are feeling a little bored. Maybe, you have been stuck inside for a while, for whatever reason, and are feeling a little restless. Grab your partner and start prepping for game time!

Before you start playing, make a snack tray with you and your partner's favorite munchies. If it's cold outside, make some homemade hot cocoa with an assortment of add-ins, like marshmallows, caramel drizzle, whipped cream, sprinkles, etc. If you're both coffee enthusiast, make a nice pour-over or French press with all the delicious additions, like flavored syrups, and an assortment of milks and creamers.

Now it's time to pull out your favorite board games. You can introduce each other to your personal favorites, or you can discover and learn to play board games that neither of you has played. You can try popular games from the world over. You can opt to play adult games, like the board game "Monogamy," "Our Moments," "Dirty Minds," "Never Have I Ever," "the Wheel of Foreplay," "I Dare You," "Sex Questions," "Get Nasty," just to name a few!

Make it a point to build your board game collection, so that on those days when you're trying to beat the boredom, you can pull out the board games and get to the loving!

Planning Notes:

Who can provide "expert" knowledge, if necessary?

_____

_____

What items do you need to bring?

_____

_____

Where will the activity take place?

_____

_____

When will the activity take place?

_____

_____

Additional Pre-activity Notes:

_____

_____

Post-Activity Notes, Ideas, & Suggestions:

_____

_____

_____

_____

_____

_____

_____

_____

_____

_____

_____

_____

_____

Activity No. 11: Notice

Grab two yellow sticky note pads; give one to your partner and keep the other for yourself. Through the course of a week, you should write a note of appreciation to your partner every time you notice them doing something noteworthy. Write an encouraging, heartfelt note to your partner, and leave the note in a place where your partner is sure to find it. Your goal is to use up every sheet of your note pad, by taking notice of the noteworthy efforts of your lover. Be vulnerable, open, encouraging, and affirming. Let your partner know how beautiful, wonderful, special, patient, kind, considerate, funny, loving, adorable, sexy, intelligent, wise, faithful, loyal, talented, praiseworthy, unique, deserving, kind, and incredible that they are!

Keep all the sticky notes that you received in a notebook, and have your partner do the same. At the end of the week, plan a candlelight dinner at home or your favorite restaurant. Take turns reading the notes that you received from your partner, and vice versa. Share how the notes made you feel, and encourage your partner to share the same. Keep your notebooks in a safe place, so that when you run into a rough patch, need reminding of how wonderful you both are to each other, or want to reminisce in the love you shared, pull out the notes, grab a bottle of bubbly, and take note!

Planning Notes:

Who can provide "expert" knowledge, if necessary?

_____

_____

What items do you need to bring?

_____

_____

Where will the activity take place?

_____

_____

When will the activity take place?

_____

_____

Additional Pre-activity Notes:

_____

_____

Post-Activity Notes, Ideas, & Suggestions:

_____

_____

_____

_____

_____

_____

_____

_____

_____

_____

_____

_____

Activity No. 12: Baby, "Train" Me

Putting away the mobile phones and any unnecessary distractions to focus on one another for any extended period can help "recalibrate" a passion-thirsty relationship, keep the intimacy of an already romantic relationship well-fueled, or put a little fire into the start of growing intimacy. A train ride can provide just the perfect romantic getaway to help train your lover to enjoy the ride. The travel channel already did the homework for you by compiling a list of the ten most romantic train rides around the globe.

If you and your lover are already in the Paris, the most romantic city in the world, then you two should take Belmond's Art Deco styled Venice Simplon-Orient-Express. If you are visiting during the month of August, you can book the road from Paris to Istanbul with stops in both Budapest and Bucharest. You can expect to enjoy a four-course gourmet meal, the famed champagne bar, and a car with a pianist. Take along romantic activities and sultry, thought-provoking conversation topics. Time to get in that training and take your romance to a whole new level.

If you are a romantic die hard, then take the most luxurious Maharajas Express in India that boasts of having the Taj Mahal as one of its destination sites. The Taj Mahal is one of most famed structures ever built: the 17th century emperor Shah Jahan built a mausoleum in memory of and homage to his wife. Enjoy the scenery with your partner, and somewhere along the route, you might see a tiger!

There is the coveted Seven Stars train ride that is only available for a lottery selected 28 passengers per trip, as there are only 14 available suites. The one and only grand suite has a floor-to-ceiling window where you and your loved one can view the picturesque landscape, which includes volcanoes, hots springs, and lush vegetation. This may take you and your love to the seventh heaven!

If you have wanted to visit the ancient city of Machu Picchu in Peru, do it the way that lovers should! Go by train, so that you can enjoy the company of your lover in a swanky 1920's Pullman with champagne and Peruvian wine service, along with delicious Peruvian dishes and Peruvian music. Hold your lover tight and whisper a loving poem in their ear. Hold hands, massage shoulders, kiss the nape of each other's necks. Ascend the Andes Mountains while falling more and more in love!

A trip to Africa is on most of our bucket lists, and even if you are fortunate enough to be from the continent, there are so many sites and cities to explore that even you still have several sites and countries to visit on your bucket list. Plan a lover's getaway on the Rovos trail that has seven routes to choose from; you can go from Capetown, South Africa, to Dar es Salaam, Tanzania. There are some exciting highlights along that route, and you can book a suite with an actual bathtub (which is a rarity on a train). Now, fall deeper in love as you enjoy the famous Kimberley Falls, one of the featured route highlights, and make use of the tub for one of those romantic tub rituals.

Lover's romantic fantasies usually include picturesque mountains, waterfalls, and beautiful beaches. You can enjoy making your fantasies a reality as you take a 35-hour Amtrak trek between Los Angeles and Seattle. Book a private room with a personal attendant, enjoy the Parlour Room, which is a classy, lovers-approved lounge that offers wine and cheese pairings, a full bar, books, board games, and a theatre.

Bring your own books that you and your partner have chosen and read side by side, if you wish.

Just try to stay on the same page! You might decide to sneak in your own risqué board games and find a secluded nook to quietly play in. What a SEXY lovers' getaway this can be!

Planning Notes:

Who can provide "expert" knowledge, if necessary?

_____

_____

What items do you need to bring?

_____

_____

Where will the activity take place?

_____

_____

When will the activity take place?

_____

_____

Additional Pre-activity Notes:

_____

_____

Post-Activity Notes, Ideas, & Suggestions:

Activity No. 13: Catch Me

There are no better fish in the sea than the one that you already have hooked, so choose to "make love" to your partner during a day spent fishing. The goal should of this activity should be more centered on bonding than on simply catching fish. If neither of you can fish, find a knowledgeable friend who has equipment that you can use, and pay them to be your guide, provided you do not mind being respectfully romantic in their company. You might, in that case, just make it a couple's day. If either one or both of you fish, then keep it simple and use the equipment that you already have—bait, hooks, and poles, along with cleaning utensils and a cooler for the catch. Bring a second cooler filled with your favorite finger foods and drinks, and that will be all you'll need. If you are fortunate to have more sophisticated gear (or even a boat), then plan and prepare!

Fishing can be a watching and waiting game where silence and quiet can be paramount. It is often a sport for solace and solitude seekers. However, the quiet and still characteristics of fishing, except for those moments where there is a catch on the line, is exactly what many couples need to reconnect. Sitting quietly, drifting slowly, and waiting patiently in one another's company, is often all that's needed to ignite a good and much-needed discourse, or allow the pair to sit and reflect on the real "catch."

There are some beautiful lakes all over the country. No matter where you live, there is certainly a fishing hole you can find to kick off a little "lovemaking!"

Planning Notes:

Who can provide "expert" knowledge, if necessary?

_____

_____

What items do you need to bring?

_____

_____

Where will the activity take place?

_____

_____

When will the activity take place?

_____

_____

Additional Pre-activity Notes:

_____

_____

Post–Activity Notes, Ideas, & Suggestions:

Activity No. 14: Chick-Flick Fest

Romantic movies (a.k.a. chick flicks and romantic comedies) can ignite warm fuzzy feelings, particularly for the feminine heart. Even if they aren't your cup of tea, you can't deny their power to put the feminine spirit in a whirlwind of wonderfully warm emotions. With that in mind, be open to selecting and purchasing an entire day's worth of chick flicks to enjoy with your partner. There should be at least a few that you'll find appealing.

Once you have established and obtained your movie list, make sure to get your viewing space nice and cozy. Plenty of comfy pillows, freshly laundered blankets sprayed with aromatic linen spray, finger foods, junk food, treats, and/or healthy eats, will ensure that you two have a grand time. Put the phones on silent and schedule intermissions for checking calls or taking momentary breaks, including bathroom breaks. Make sure to incorporate plenty of cuddling, kissing, and fondling!

Series Overdose

You can "make love" to your significant other during an overdosing on a popular television series. Find an appropriate series (preferably one that has some sexy, sultry, romantic, nude, or risqué scenes) that neither of you have watched but are both interested in. Set the stage, set the tone, and set the mood. Kiss, feel, touch, fondle, nibble, lick, hug, hold, rub, and most of all—BOND!

Planning Notes:

Who can provide "expert" knowledge, if necessary?

_____

_____

What items do you need to bring?

_____

_____

Where will the activity take place?

_____

_____

When will the activity take place?

_____

_____

Additional Pre-activity Notes:

_____

_____

Post-Activity Notes, Ideas, & Suggestions:

مكاني المفضل هو معك.

Activity No. 15: Dicktionary

If you have ever heard the term "live and learn," let's change it to "love and learn." Grab two dictionaries: one for you, and one for your partner, and make sure that you have the same exact one. You and your partner should start with the first word of the dictionary and go word-by-word, trying to use the words in sexy, sultry, provocative, naughty, romantic, and sexually-charged sentences. Keep it light, keep it tasteful, keep it fun, but most of all...keep it going! Try to make sure you get in a few good laughs. Like every other occasion, set the mood with good drinks and good food!

Mark where you stop so that you can resume at any time. Hopefully, you will eventually make it through the entire dictionary and add new words to your vocabulary—words that I'm certain you'll never forget!

Planning Notes:

Who can provide "expert" knowledge, if necessary?

_____

_____

What items do you need to bring?

_____

_____

Where will the activity take place?

_____

_____

When will the activity take place?

_____

_____

Additional Pre-activity Notes:

_____

_____

Post-Activity Notes, Ideas, & Suggestions:

_____

_____

_____

_____

_____

_____

_____

_____

_____

_____

_____

_____

_____

Activity No. 16: Eat Me

You have your favorite dishes, and so does your mate, but can you prepare them from scratch? Why not demonstrate your love for each other by taking professional cooking classes together, where you learn how to make your lover's favorite meal, and your lover does the same for you? Devote yourself to perfecting the techniques necessary to make the meal superbly. Set a dinner date and show off your skills! Make sure to have nice place settings, candles, wine, bubbly, and flowers!

Nyotaimori

Nyotaimori is the Japanese art of eating sushi off the body of a naked woman. You and your lover can adapt this artistry at home. You can pick up sushi from a local restaurant; some grocery stores offer freshly made sushi as well. Grab some sake and matcha tea for drinks, and for dessert, you can pick up some ice cream or try Japanese mochi if you're feeling adventurous.

One of you can start first by allowing your partner to dine from your freshly-bathed and sweet-smelling body. Afterwards, your partner will allow you to partake by offering their body to you in a similar manner. To clean up, you both can partake in a bathing ritual, if you like.

Go to the next level by offering your lover your body for a dessert tray, and your partner will do the same for you afterwards. You can end the entire dining experience with a shower ritual.

Planning Notes:

Who can provide "expert" knowledge, if necessary?

_____

_____

What items do you need to bring?

_____

_____

Where will the activity take place?

_____

_____

When will the activity take place?

_____

_____

Additional Pre-activity Notes:

_____

_____

Post-Activity Notes, Ideas, & Suggestions:

_____

_____

_____

_____

_____

_____

_____

_____

_____

_____

_____

_____

_____

Me encantas tal y
como eres...

Activity No. 17: Birthday Suit Paint

Instead of having dessert after a romantic lunch or dinner, you and your partner can make edible paint and have a body painting party. Make sure to properly prep your play area to avoid paint getting anywhere that you do not want it. You can play on an inexpensive shower curtain or liner, an old sheet or blanket, etc.

You will need the following supplies:

1. Little tiny plastic cups
2. Food coloring in all your favorite colors (you can mix colors to make new ones)
3. 2 tablespoons of sugar
4. ⅓ cup of cornstarch
5. Optional flavoring extracts like vanilla, almond, lemon

Directions:

1. Place the sugar and cornstarch in a medium pan on medium heat.
2. Write the name of each color you're planning to use on the mini plastic cups, and line them up side by side.
3. Watch carefully as you slowly cook, making sure to watch as the liquid transforms from a cloudy mixture to a clear, translucent gel.
4. Put a few drops of the corresponding food color into each cup.
5. Add the sugar gel to each cup.

6. Mix the containers of each cup, adding more food coloring or gel as needed to get the perfect color.
7. Allow to cool.

Now it's time for you and your partner to get into your birthday suits. Use your fingers to paint designs onto your partner, then remove the paint with moist, tender kisses. Kiss every centimeter of your partner's body: use a ruler, if necessary, so you do not miss any part!

Planning Notes:

Who can provide "expert" knowledge, if necessary?

_____

_____

What items do you need to bring?

_____

_____

Where will the activity take place?

_____

_____

When will the activity take place?

_____

_____

Additional Pre-activity Notes:

_____

_____

Post-Activity Notes, Ideas, & Suggestions:

Activity No. 18: Love Language

Each of us has a love language—the language that tells us that we are loved. There are five general love languages; in some cases, couples do not share the same love language, which can lead to frustration. We often show love in the language that we comprehend, but our partner may not comprehend it nor express it in the same language. To make sure that your love communication is effective, it is best to understand both of your love languages, so that you can express love in the way that your partner best understands it, and vice versa.

The five love languages:
1. Words of Affirmation
2. Acts of Service
3. Physical Touch
4. Gift Giving
5. Quality Time

You can purchase Dr. Chapman's book, "The 5 Love Languages," to get a deeper understanding of these love languages. You can also choose to take their test online, download the app, or do all three.

Set the stage, as usual! By now, you know what to do! Get the bubbly, the smoothies, the chocolates, the chips, the cheese, the nuts, the fruit, or prepare a full candlelight dinner. You might decide to hire a chef to come to you! The main purpose is to decide what you and your partner might enjoy as you get to know one another on a deeper level. Visit the website at *www.5lovelanguages.com*.

Planning Notes:

Who can provide "expert" knowledge, if necessary?

_____

_____

What items do you need to bring?

_____

_____

Where will the activity take place?

_____

_____

When will the activity take place?

_____

_____

Additional Pre-activity Notes:

_____

_____

Post-Activity Notes, Ideas, & Suggestions:

_____

_____

_____

_____

_____

_____

_____

_____

_____

_____

_____

_____

_____

_____

Activity No. 19: The Rub Down

After a hard or stressful day for your partner, one of the best ways to help them relax is to run your lover's bath water and allow them to relax inside. Make a soothing, warming drink or cocktail, and bring it to them in the tub. Don't rush this process—focus on their relaxation.

When your partner is ready to exit the tub, have a warmed robe ready for them by simply tumble drying it. Guide your partner to bed, have them lie down, and help them relax as you rub them down with warmed shea butter, lotion, or massage oil from head to toe. Make sure that the lights have been dimmed, the aromatherapy candles lit, and the soft relaxing sounds of jazz, classical, or your favorite tunes are playing in the background.

Rub and stoke! Rub and cup! Rub and caress! Rub and kiss! Rub and lick! Rub and squeeze! Rub and nibble! Rub and...pinch? Rub and...bite?! Whatever you do, make sure that your partner is okay with it beforehand.

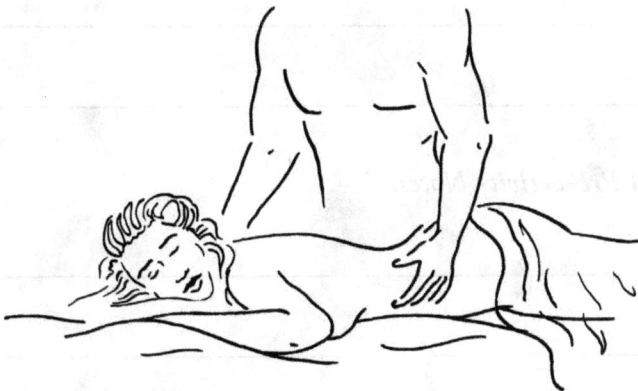

Planning Notes:

Who can provide "expert" knowledge, if necessary?

_____

_____

What items do you need to bring?

_____

_____

Where will the activity take place?

_____

_____

When will the activity take place?

_____

_____

Additional Pre-activity Notes:

_____

_____

Post-Activity Notes, Ideas, & Suggestions:

Activity No. 20: National Park Pact

One of the fondest memories that I have is taking the 8+ hour ride on a beautiful sunny day through Yellowstone National Park. To maintain the sanctity of the parks, many national parks don't have cell towers, which forces you to put your phone away and focus on your partner and the scenery. Many parks offer activities, from swimming, hiking, and fishing, to rafting and kayaking. Most offer camping options as well, whether via motorhome or tent.

When spending a day in nature, remember to pack plenty of snacks and drinks—you'll need them! You may decide to pack a picnic of your favorite foods and stop by a stream, lake, or waterfall, and take respite. The beauty, serenity, and animals in their habitat are all elements that induce peaceful and amorous feelings. Make sure to dive into some of your deepest discussions, share your deepest feelings, or read romantic and erotic poems aloud. Stop and steal a kiss, snag a hug, do a little fondling, perform a minute-massage, and don't forget to take bathroom breaks!

Discover the parks:
- *Acadia* in Maine
- *Arches* in Utah
- *Cuyahoga* in Ohio
- *Glacier* in Montana
- *The Grand Canyon* in Arizona
- *Grand Teton* in Wyoming
- *The Great Smoky Mountains* in Tennessee and North Carolina
- *Kenai Fjords* in Alaska

- *Olympic National* in Washington
- *Rocky Mountain National* in Colorado
- *Yellowstone National* in Wyoming
- *Yosemite* in California

Planning Notes:

Who can provide "expert" knowledge, if necessary?

_____

_____

What items do you need to bring?

_____

_____

Where will the activity take place?

_____

_____

When will the activity take place?

_____

_____

Additional Pre-activity Notes:

_____

_____

Post–Activity Notes, Ideas, & Suggestions:

_____

_____

_____

_____

_____

_____

_____

_____

_____

_____

_____

_____

Activity No. 21: Prince Playlist Purple Passion Party

Prince has some of the most suggestive, sultry, erotic, and sexy songs ever recorded. If you aren't familiar with his songs, the titles are good indicators of the raciness of the lyrics. Since purple was known to be his color, celebrate this activity in hues of purple.

Create a purple cocktail. Make some lavender lemonade, cupcakes with lavender-laced icing, a pretty purple kale salad, or a Thai purple coleslaw salad. Use blueberries and beet juice to make natural food coloring, which can be added to all kinds of dishes to give them hues of purple. Make a pathway of petals into the house, and make sure that the lights are dimmed. Get a blanket, comfy pillows, and massage oil, and sit your partner down for a wildly erotic playlist. Here are some suggestions, but bear in mind—these songs are XXX!

Prince Purple Playlist:
- *Insatiable*
- *Adore*
- *Scandalous*
- *Purple Rain*
- *Kiss*
- *Orgasm*
- *Sexy MF*
- *Delirious*
- *Do it All Night*
- *Sex in the Summer*

- *Erotic City*
- *Soft n' Wet*
- *I Wanna Be Your Lover*
- *Darling Nikki*
- *If I Was Your Girlfriend*
- *Little Red Corvette*
- *Head*
- *Jack U Off*
- *Come*
- *P Control*
- *Sugar Walls*
- *Get Off*

Planning Notes:

Who can provide "expert" knowledge, if necessary?

_____

_____

What items do you need to bring?

_____

_____

Where will the activity take place?

_____

_____

When will the activity take place?

_____

_____

Additional Pre-activity Notes:

_____

_____

Post–Activity Notes, Ideas, & Suggestions:

_____

_____

_____

_____

_____

_____

_____

_____

_____

_____

_____

Activity No. 22: Body Care Concocting Class

What better way to add your own twist to water rituals than to use products that you and your lover have crafted together? If there isn't an actual class you can take, scour YouTube for inspiration, since there are plenty of amazing DIY YouTubers who can show you their handiwork. Always set your stage with edible delights that turn you both on and up, like your favorite wine, champagne, finger foods, exotic delicacies, mini pastries, etc. Purchase a complete list of your necessary ingredients beforehand. Create your romantic playlist. Have your YouTube teachers ready on demand and make custom shampoo, detangler, body wash, body butter, massage oils, or all of the above!

Try my favorite sites for recipes, instructions, supplies, and ideas:
- From Nature, With Love
- Mountain Rose Herbs
- DIY Lotioncrafters
- Bulk Apothecary
- Liberty Naturals

Together, you can create sensual and naughty names for your products. You can use them the same day/evening, or you can wait to use them after a full day of water play. If you make your own signature fragrances, every time you and your partner wear your love elixirs and concoctions, you'll be reminded of the wonderful moments you shared creating your soft, creamy, and luxurious passion potions!

Planning Notes:

Who can provide "expert" knowledge, if necessary?

_____

_____

What items do you need to bring?

_____

_____

Where will the activity take place?

_____

_____

When will the activity take place?

_____

_____

Additional Pre-activity Notes:

_____

_____

Post-Activity Notes, Ideas, & Suggestions:

Activity No. 23: Wine Tasting

Wine is considered to be the elixir for lovers, so you and your partner should go experience a wine tasting course together.

There are some beautiful wineries and outright gorgeous vineyards both here in the United States and all around the world! California has beautiful wine country with so many amazing options, and you can even tour Napa Valley via a wine train. Wine can put you in a wonderfully romantic mood. Set the stage with chocolates, flowers, essential oils, and enjoy the atmosphere!

When you have completed your wine tasting, make sure to purchase a few of your favorite bottles to take back home. Pull out your latex sheets or use a plastic shower curtain and prepare to do a "nice and naughty" wine tasting, starting with your partner's navel—sip and kiss! Go from head to toe: pour a little, lick a little, taste a little, sip a little!

Planning Notes:

Who can provide "expert" knowledge, if necessary?

_____

_____

What items do you need to bring?

_____

_____

Where will the activity take place?

_____

_____

When will the activity take place?

_____

_____

Additional Pre-activity Notes:

_____

_____

Post-Activity Notes, Ideas, & Suggestions:

Activity No. 24: Tattooed for You

I don't think that anyone should tattoo the name or likeness of a mate onto their bodies. However, if you and/or your mate wish to ink your bodies, it can be an opportunity to bond. Working together to create your tattoos with your tattoo artist is an artistic adventure. I would suggest that you and your mate create pieces unique to each of you. Scour through books, magazines, photographs, and artwork to find inspiration. Doodle and draw together. Explore the internet; check the website and Instagram accounts of renowned artists. Educate yourselves on styles and techniques. Once you have concrete ideas and are certain of the tattoo artist(s) that you both want to work with, then set your appointments. Make sure to visit as many parlors and artists as possible so that you can make sure you like their vibe.

On the day of your appointments, avoid caffeine and alcohol: both can cause increased blood flow, which isn't ideal. Dress comfortably, and purchase your aftercare regimen in advance. If you have separate artists and are scheduled at the same time, you can video chat each other in the process. If you're wanting your partner present during the appointment, then there should be plenty of moments for a hand squeeze of support, a soft kiss of encouragement, a gentle rub of comfort, a simple nod of approval, or some loving words. All of these will help ease the "pain" and make the process all the more memorable.

After each of you has completed your tattoos, your artwork will require care. Aid your partner by cleaning and applying ointment to it, as is advised by your artist. This is a loving gesture. Bear in mind, however, that tattoos can be addictive.

Planning Notes:

Who can provide "expert" knowledge, if necessary?

_____

_____

What items do you need to bring?

_____

_____

Where will the activity take place?

_____

_____

When will the activity take place?

_____

_____

Additional Pre-activity Notes:

_____

_____

Post-Activity Notes, Ideas, & Suggestions:

_____

_____

_____

_____

_____

_____

_____

_____

_____

_____

_____

_____

_____

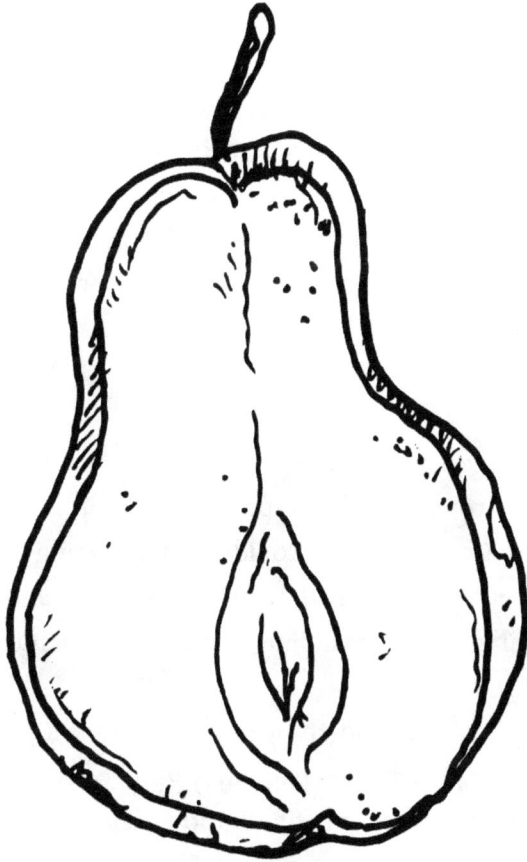

Ich bin bis über beide
Ohren verliebt.

Activity No. 25: Tell Me A Secret

A real testament to your bond with your partner is your desire, willingness, and inclination to unveil yourself—to get "naked" in their presence and freely be your authentic self. You need to feel comfortable sharing your truth—the good, the bad, the pretty, the ugly, the obvious, and yes, even the SECRETS! Each of us has secrets in all categories.

Rules of Engagement:
1.   Don't share secrets that expose other people.
2.   Don't share secrets that could end up hurting someone else.
3.   Share secrets that are likely to bring you and your partner closer, like feelings of vulnerability, desires, ideas, stances, emotions.

Set the stage. Maybe you enjoy tequila, so take a shot before each secret to loosen up. Maybe you two enjoy good coffee, so make a good French Press and set up your coffee station. Take long sips before and after your stories. You may enjoy wine, hot tea, or refreshing beverages. Whatever the two of you enjoy, have it available and romantically staged. Also, have a box of Kleenex available. There are likely to be some tears.

Most importantly, be a safe haven for your partner. Wherever we believe our secrets are safe, we are more likely to leave our hearts in the same place.

Planning Notes:

Who can provide "expert" knowledge, if necessary?

_____

_____

What items do you need to bring?

_____

_____

Where will the activity take place?

_____

_____

When will the activity take place?

_____

_____

Additional Pre-activity Notes:

_____

_____

Post-Activity Notes, Ideas, & Suggestions:

_____

_____

_____

_____

_____

_____

_____

_____

_____

_____

_____

_____

Activity No. 26: Be A Kid Again

Back in the day, I "fell in love" with a boy at eleven years old. It wasn't based on physical contact; I was mesmerized by how he rode his dirt bike and how much fun he and his friends were having. He had piercing eyes and a serious stare, but at the same time, the biggest smile and loudest laugh. He was chock full of antics, jokes, and ideas for playing pranks, teasing me and my best friend. Most of all, though, I loved how easy it was to have plain ol' fun. So now, it's your turn!

Get out the bikes, skates, old school board games, water guns, water hose, bubbles, jacks, jumbo chalk, UNO cards, tic tac toe, hopscotch, double Dutch rope, cartoons, and movies you enjoyed as a kid. Find your favorite childhood treats, create the playlist that was the soundtrack of your childhoods, and KID OUT! The biggest treat is that now, you should be old enough to either give the kiss you used to sneak or receive the kiss that made you run away with butterflies from your tummy to the tips of your toes!

Planning Notes:

Who can provide "expert" knowledge, if necessary?

_____

_____

What items do you need to bring?

_____

_____

Where will the activity take place?

_____

_____

When will the activity take place?

_____

_____

Additional Pre-activity Notes:

_____

_____

Post-Activity Notes, Ideas, & Suggestions:

_____

_____

_____

_____

_____

_____

_____

_____

_____

_____

_____

_____

Activity No. 27: Floral Arranging

The way to many lovers' hearts is with the gifting of beautiful floral bouquets, aromatic herbs, and beautiful household plants. Their aroma, their myriad of colors, their giving of so much joy, reminds us of the beauty of nature. These qualities, and the fact that they can require so little effort, are just some of the reasons why flowers are so powerful.

You and your partner can opt to take a floral arranging class together, where you can learn which flowers are available during what time of the year, and which states, regions, and countries offer the most and best options. You'll be able to experience flowers that you have never experienced before—seeing their beauty, smelling their fragrance, feeling their petals. Some are edible and make wonderful teas, jellies, candies, and additions to cocktails and herbal infusions. You two might discover some new favorite flowers along the way!

Learn how to arrange these flowers to suit your home decor, for your partner's taste, or for moments when you would like to surprise your partner with the gift of flowers. I hope you will make flower giving a regular surprise in your partner's life. They are beautiful on an office desk, a bathroom windowsill, a kitchen counter, a bedroom dresser, anywhere!

Planning Notes:

Who can provide "expert" knowledge, if necessary?

_____

_____

What items do you need to bring?

_____

_____

Where will the activity take place?

_____

_____

When will the activity take place?

_____

_____

Additional Pre-activity Notes:

_____

_____

Post-Activity Notes, Ideas, & Suggestions:

_____

_____

_____

_____

_____

_____

_____

_____

_____

_____

_____

_____

Não consigo parar de
pensar em você...

Activity No. 28: Number 1 Fan

Find just the perfect occasion to go "all-out" to demonstrate that you are your sweetheart's number one fan and most devoted cheerleader. You might find this moment if your partner is a sports enthusiast, enjoys playing sports, plays on an organized team, enjoys going to sporting events, or loves hosting events. Sport the garb, wear the colors, wave the banners, shake the pom-poms, and plan an all-out victory party.

If your lover is a performer of any sort, show up with a host of friends to lend support, clap wildly, and demonstrate unparalleled enthusiasm and excitement. Bring the appropriate token of recognition; just make sure you go above and beyond!

As a bonus round, end the evening with your lover's favorite rituals!

Planning Notes:

Who can provide "expert" knowledge, if necessary?

_____

_____

What items do you need to bring?

_____

_____

Where will the activity take place?

_____

_____

When will the activity take place?

_____

_____

Additional Pre-activity Notes:

_____

_____

Post–Activity Notes, Ideas, & Suggestions:

_____

_____

_____

_____

_____

_____

_____

_____

_____

_____

_____

_____

_____

Activity No. 29: Origami Love Notes

Why not take an origami class online or find an origami master on YouTube who's offering free demonstrations and instructions? Now, take it one step further: purchase packs of fancy Chiyogami and plain Unryu mulberry paper that you and your lover can decorate and embellish by hand. Purchase watercolor pens and markers. You can order online from Amazon, an art supply store, or you can make a trip to your local Michael's, MJ Designs, Hobby Lobby, or Walmart.

As usual, set the stage with snacks you both enjoy. Set the mood with a playlist you both love. Clear a table and arrange your laptop, all of your art supplies, and whatever else you might need. Decorate your paper with love notes. Think of all the witty, wordy ways to express your love. Find quotes, look up Biblical scriptures, recount special memories, write a poem—just express yourself.

Once you both have made all your love-note papers, then you can begin constructing and folding the paper into wonderful works of art. After you have completed your pieces, you can trade, read, and re-fold. Show your appreciation by unwrapping yourself emotionally (and physically), and by folding your fears, reservations, and clothes neatly in a corner. Embrace the words, embrace your partner, and unfold the kisses, the caressing, the romance!

Keep your lover's notes. Place them in special spots in your surroundings to remind you of how much you are treasured and loved.

Planning Notes:

Who can provide "expert" knowledge, if necessary?

_____

_____

What items do you need to bring?

_____

_____

Where will the activity take place?

_____

_____

When will the activity take place?

_____

_____

Additional Pre-activity Notes:

_____

_____

Post-Activity Notes, Ideas, & Suggestions:

Activity No. 30: Custom Lingerie Shopping & Fitting

Most undergarments fit poorly and are produced for the masses, so you and your lover should go shopping for custom-made lingerie. There is nothing better than having the garments that lay closest to the body fit that body precisely—this is amplified when donning a nice outfit. Nothing is sexier than seeing a loved one in a nicely fitted robe, negligee, panties, or briefs that accentuates the custom curves of those intimate body parts, or a custom-fitted brassiere that cups the breast, ever so perfectly.

Planning Notes:

Who can provide "expert" knowledge, if necessary?

_____

_____

What items do you need to bring?

_____

_____

Where will the activity take place?

_____

_____

When will the activity take place?

_____

_____

Additional Pre-activity Notes:

_____

_____

Post-Activity Notes, Ideas, & Suggestions:

_____

_____

_____

_____

_____

_____

_____

_____

_____

_____

_____

_____

_____

Activity No. 31: Laundering Lingerie Day

You and your partner can take good care of your intimate apparel by laundering them together. Go through your drawers together and discard old undergarments: those that are discolored, stretched out, ill-fitting, torn, or overly worn. Allow your mate to choose the ones to keep! Once you've decided on the keepers, prepare to wash them all together.

Do not settle on store purchased laundry detergent. Make your own organic option with you and your mate's signature scent. I love the aroma of sandalwood: that woodsy, musky scent never fails to put me in an amorous mood. Find essential oils that do the same for you and your partner. You may enjoy rose, orange, lavender, patchouli, vetiver, ylang-ylang, anise, geranium, etc. Explore and experiment to create a unique scent for your intimate apparel. You can make satchets for your dresser drawers as well.

After you and your partner complete the washing of your garments, you should fold your partners undies, and have your partner fold yours. Carefully and lovingly put away each one, folding and arranging them so that your sachets are nestled abundantly amongst your "love-laced" garments. I bet you remembered to have the stage set and the mood music mix playing "in stereo!"

Planning Notes:

Who can provide "expert" knowledge, if necessary?

_____

_____

What items do you need to bring?

_____

_____

Where will the activity take place?

_____

_____

When will the activity take place?

_____

_____

Additional Pre-activity Notes:

_____

_____

Post-Activity Notes, Ideas, & Suggestions:

_____

_____

_____

_____

_____

_____

_____

_____

_____

_____

_____

_____

_____

Activity No. 32: That Time of Month

Whenever a woman is involved, there's most likely going to be a time of the month. For many partners, it's considered a trying time because menstruation can create changes in a woman's body that can contribute to mood swings, irritability, lethargy, and food cravings. Do not allow this monthly occurrence get the best of you and your partner. Instead, use it to make love...to show love.

Beforehand, make an effort to learn about all of the sanitary options available nowadays: there are tampons, pads, reusable cups, disks, and more. Learn about and discuss them all, finding out what your partner uses and prefers. When the time comes, make sure to have all sanitary supplies on deck. Set the stage, but this stage might require different options. Find out what your partner needs. Maybe a certain tea, particular pain relief medication, certain food cravings, heating pad, specific bedding, and undergarments for mishaps. Your partner's mood may be different from normal, so instead of the normal sexy playlist, your partner may prefer a different, more calming one.

Know that your partner's emotions can be triggered more easily, so be mindful of the stimuli you choose during this time. If your partner suffers from PMS, try to keep the stimuli as neutral as possible to not to evoke an emotional outburst. This is such a wonderful time to give and receive love. Make sure there is an emergency "period care kit" in every automobile and of your abodes if you live separately.

Planning Notes:

Who can provide "expert" knowledge, if necessary?

_____

_____

What items do you need to bring?

_____

_____

Where will the activity take place?

_____

_____

When will the activity take place?

_____

_____

Additional Pre-activity Notes:

_____

_____

Post-Activity Notes, Ideas, & Suggestions:

_____

_____

_____

_____

_____

_____

_____

_____

_____

_____

_____

_____

_____

Activity No. 33: Kitty & Ditty Care

Feminine hygiene can be a little bit more complicated than masculine hygiene. The pH balance of the vagina needs to be between 3.8 to 4.5; douching, using scented products or deodorants down there, changes in hormone levels, taking antibiotics, and a poor diet can all throw off this delicate balance; When that occurs, the vagina can become uncomfortable and emit a foul odor.

Sit down with your partner and have a kitty and ditty care discussion. Learn about and/or teach your partner about proper kitty/ditty care. If you or your partner have questions, you can always find credible sources on the internet with sound advice. Be willing to investigate your body, allow your partner to investigate your body, and vice versa. Ask for feedback and provide feedback of your own. I'm sure that you want to smell fresh, and you want your partner to smell fresh as well, so learn to discuss this topic openly!

Planning Notes:

Who can provide "expert" knowledge, if necessary?

_____

_____

What items do you need to bring?

_____

_____

Where will the activity take place?

_____

_____

When will the activity take place?

_____

_____

Additional Pre-activity Notes:

_____

_____

Post-Activity Notes, Ideas, & Suggestions:

_____

_____

_____

_____

_____

_____

_____

_____

_____

_____

_____

_____

_____

私にはあなたがいるので、
夢は要りません

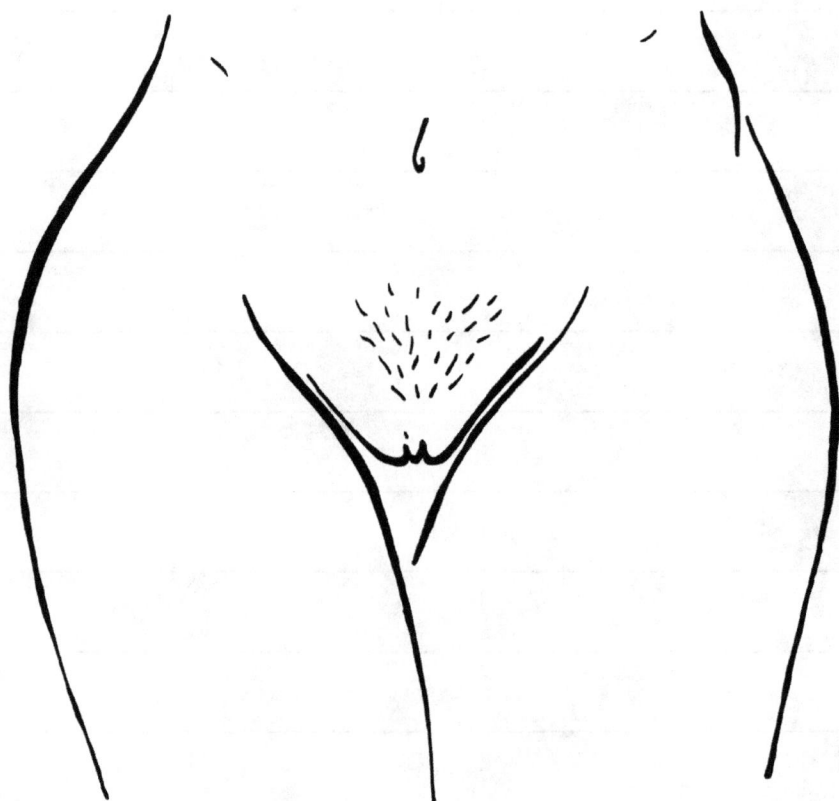

Activity No. 34: Let's Go Brazilian

Spend a day enjoying a wax ritual with your partner; there are many more options than just the Brazilian. Start by finding a reputable salon for you and your partner; some salons cater to women, and others cater to men who undergo a different process.

Discuss with your partner beforehand how each of you wants the other waxed. You can research many different styles online. Take the time to look over the options prior to your appointments and make sure the salon you select can provide the services you desire. Have fun going down the smooth and silky path!

Planning Notes:

Who can provide "expert" knowledge, if necessary?

_____

_____

What items do you need to bring?

_____

_____

Where will the activity take place?

_____

_____

When will the activity take place?

_____

_____

Additional Pre-activity Notes:

_____

_____

Post-Activity Notes, Ideas, & Suggestions:

Activity No. 35: Kiss My Teeth

I just love how my teeth feel after a good dental cleaning. I cannot stop running my tongue across my pearly whites and feeling the slick smoothness. Good dental hygiene is downright sexy: clean white teeth, healthy gums, and fresh breath are all attractive.

Schedule a dental checkup for yourself and your partner. Maybe you go to different dentists, but that shouldn't be a problem. If you or your mate don't have a regular dentist, there are always amazing Groupons for dental examinations and cleaning. Get those pearly whites cleaned. Afterward, spend all day kissing and smiling at one another!

Planning Notes:

Who can provide "expert" knowledge, if necessary?

_____

_____

What items do you need to bring?

_____

_____

Where will the activity take place?

_____

_____

When will the activity take place?

_____

_____

Additional Pre-activity Notes:

_____

_____

Post-Activity Notes, Ideas, & Suggestions:

Activity No. 36: The Sitter

Making love to your partner is much more than just a physical act, and occasionally, it can be even more powerful when performed in the absence of your partner. One of the most demonstrative ways you can show your partner love is in the act of "sitting" for them. It is an act of service that can demonstrate your love for them by caring for someone or something that your mate loves, cherishes, treasures, and/or values.

If it is a child, parent, or family member that you are "sitting," take notes carefully. Follow all instructions. Do not leave your trusted post to anyone else. Always request permission, if and when, there is a deviation from the plan, and look for EVERY opportunity to go above and beyond. Provide better care than anticipated! If it is an apartment, home, workspace, or other such property, leave it cleaner and neater than when your partner asked for you to care for it. Always obtain permission to make ANY changes or improvements, no matter how small. You may seek permission in advance. Painting a room for your mate while house-sitting might be ideal. Perhaps, cutting the lawn or potting some plants might be a desired treat as well. What about organizing that garage or that office? Whatever you are sitting, leave him/her/them/it in some way better than before.

When your lover returns to take possession of his/her belongings, greet them with a token of love: a bag of treats delivered by the loved one/ones you've sat for, a bottle of wine left on a kitchen counter, a vase of flowers left on an office desk, a bottle of perfume/cologne left in a bathroom cabinet, or a sweet love letter left on a pillow.

Planning Notes:

Who can provide "expert" knowledge, if necessary?

_____

_____

What items do you need to bring?

_____

_____

Where will the activity take place?

_____

_____

When will the activity take place?

_____

_____

Additional Pre-activity Notes:

_____

_____

Post-Activity Notes, Ideas, & Suggestions:

Activity No. 37: Counseling Couch

Making "healthy" love is one of the most precious gifts that you can share with your mate. Willingness to go through counseling together to address any past and present issues that could present problems in your love life is a priceless show of love. Counseling can help you and your partner get to the core of any problems that might create discord. If you two are "healthy," a counseling session may be good just to help you and your *amor* plan for the future.

Planning Notes:

Who can provide "expert" knowledge, if necessary?

_____

_____

What items do you need to bring?

_____

_____

Where will the activity take place?

_____

_____

When will the activity take place?

_____

_____

Additional Pre-activity Notes:

_____

_____

Post-Activity Notes, Ideas, & Suggestions:

_____

_____

_____

_____

_____

_____

_____

_____

_____

_____

_____

_____

_____

Activity No. 38: Kissing Game

You should be open to learning exactly how your partner desires to be kissed and to teaching your partner exactly how you desire to be kissed. As always, set the stage and put those lips to work!

Add some tasty twists to the mix: mints, hard candies, honey on the tip of the tongue, slivers of candied ginger, chocolate kisses. Pass the treats back and forth as you kiss! Take a licorice rope with both of you starting on either end and chewing until you make it to the point where both your lips meet; when they do, go wild with kissing! Do the same with a chocolate bar, a cookie, a thin slice of cake, an ice cream sandwich, or a stick of bubble gum.

Planning Notes:

Who can provide "expert" knowledge, if necessary?

_____

_____

What items do you need to bring?

_____

_____

Where will the activity take place?

_____

_____

When will the activity take place?

_____

_____

Additional Pre-activity Notes:

_____

_____

Post-Activity Notes, Ideas, & Suggestions:

Activity No. 39: Plant a Garden

It matters not how little space you have; you and your boo can still plant a garden. You can do it with an acre or more of land, on the quaint porch of a small cottage home, on the balcony of a high-rise, or as a miniature herb garden in the window of a small college dormitory. You can decide to plant an array of fruit trees, an heirloom vegetable garden, an assortment of wildflowers, a variety of roses, a gang of edible "weeds," or your favorite herbs. The love and nurturing that you provide your garden should reflect the love and nurturing you and your partner demonstrate toward one another. Once the "fruits" from your labor of love can be harvested, it will be such a marvelous testimony to your love and devotion.

Can you imagine sipping freshly-made lemonade from the lemons of the tree that you and your lover planted? Can you taste the juiciness of those sun-ripened heirloom tomatoes in the salad you made together? Will it not be a nice surprise to hand your lover a bouquet of freshly-picked roses from the rose garden that you planted together? How nice would it be to gather the petals of all the fragrant flowers you planted together and enjoy them in a bathing ritual?

Planning Notes:

Who can provide "expert" knowledge, if necessary?

_____

_____

What items do you need to bring?

_____

_____

Where will the activity take place?

_____

_____

When will the activity take place?

_____

_____

Additional Pre-activity Notes:

_____

_____

Post-Activity Notes, Ideas, & Suggestions:

_____

_____

_____

_____

_____

_____

_____

_____

_____

_____

_____

_____

_____

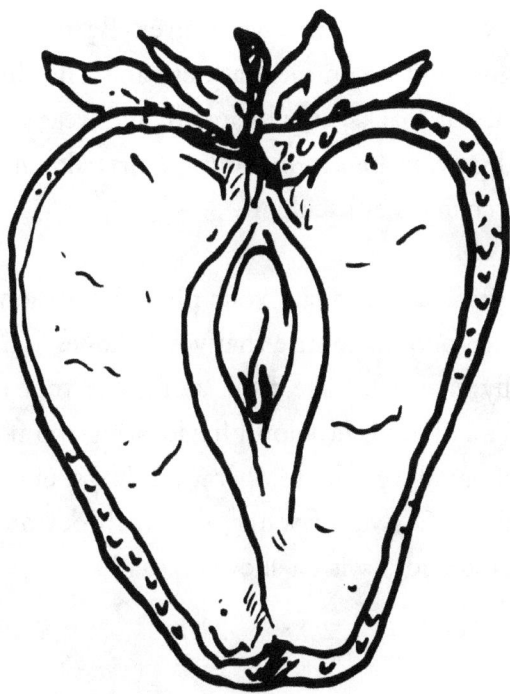

Activity No. 40: Hiking Trip

A hiking excursion is a wonderful way to build camaraderie, a healthy body, and enhanced stamina. There are trails for beginners to experts in or near almost every city on the globe! Find a trail suitable for you and your partner's levels. Choose the lower of the two levels, so that neither of you over-exert yourselves. Be mindful of weather, regulations, signs, and recommendations, and only hike established trails. Take plenty of snacks, stay hydrated, and wear appropriate gear. Have additional gear on hand, including a first aid emergency kit, in case of weather changes or accidents.

Leave your itinerary or share your phone's location with a friend or family member, and make sure that your phones and extra portable charger are fully charged. Take time along the trail to steal a kiss, snap a photo, do a live story (helpful for locating you if an unexpected incident occurs), cuddle as the temperature drops, enjoy the bliss and the beauty, and take a swig of water or crunch out on a protein bar. Enjoy the day, and end it with a shower ritual!

Planning Notes:

Who can provide "expert" knowledge, if necessary?

_____

_____

What items do you need to bring?

_____

_____

Where will the activity take place?

_____

_____

When will the activity take place?

_____

_____

Additional Pre-activity Notes:

_____

_____

Post-Activity Notes, Ideas, & Suggestions:

_____

_____

_____

_____

_____

_____

_____

_____

_____

_____

_____

_____

_____

Activity No. 41: Helicopter Ride

Plan a helicopter getaway for you and your 'lovely one." Some routes can take you over mountains, beaches, and famous landmarks. You can look for an excursion that lands on a mountaintop, where you can make a toast, take photographs, or even have a romantic lunch. There are also options to a beach-front for a toast, a picnic, or a quick skinny dip! Enjoy the ride, and make sure to do as much kissing and cuddling as possible.

Planning Notes:

Who can provide "expert" knowledge, if necessary?

_____

_____

What items do you need to bring?

_____

_____

Where will the activity take place?

_____

_____

When will the activity take place?

_____

_____

Additional Pre-activity Notes:

_____

_____

Post-Activity Notes, Ideas, & Suggestions:

Activity No. 42: Boat Ride

The amount of fun a twosome can have in a boat is limitless. You can take a ride in a trolling boat, stop mid-river and just enjoy the scenery, each other, and "make out." You can take a speedboat and jet across a river at full speed for a thrill. The two of you can plan a motorboat ride where you and your partner can do some kissing, fondling, and "motor-boating" mid-bay. You can rent a small yacht and plan a private romantic dinner cruise. Whatever you decide, set the stage, establish the mood, and monitor the tone.

Planning Notes:

Who can provide "expert" knowledge, if necessary?

_____

_____

What items do you need to bring?

_____

_____

Where will the activity take place?

_____

_____

When will the activity take place?

_____

_____

Additional Pre-activity Notes:

_____

_____

Post–Activity Notes, Ideas, & Suggestions:

_____

_____

_____

_____

_____

_____

_____

_____

_____

_____

_____

_____

Activity No. 43: Knitted Together

Why not try your hand at knitting or crocheting with your partner? You can enroll in a class or take a shot at learning online. You can establish knitting & crochet dates where you craft an item while bingeing on a series you've both wanted to watch. You could set a date and just listen to your favorite playlists and talk. You could each make squares and over time knit/crochet your squares together to make a quilt perfect for cuddling together on the sofa or taking on picnics. You could establish a knitting/crochet ritual where each square commemorates a special moment for the two of you.

When you bring all your squares together to create a wonderful memory quilt, you will be reminded of the way your lives are knitted together, quite literally.

Planning Notes:

Who can provide "expert" knowledge, if necessary?

_____

_____

What items do you need to bring?

_____

_____

Where will the activity take place?

_____

_____

When will the activity take place?

_____

_____

Additional Pre-activity Notes:

_____

_____

Post-Activity Notes, Ideas, & Suggestions:

Je t'aime pour toujours...

Activity No. 44: Fantasy Wedding

Whether you're already married or looking forward to getting married, the reality is that most of us can't afford the wedding of our dreams. However, that should not stop us from tying the knot or working hard to realize our dream as best as we can. Take an afternoon and give yourself and your partner permission to dream, to remove all limits, and to create your fantasy wedding. Make it fun. Make it fabulous. After all, it's free! Scour the internet for info. Flip through luxury magazines for inspiration. Scroll through Instagram for inspiration. By now, you know to set the stage, establish the tone and monitor the mood!

Ask yourselves...
- Where in the world would you have your wedding?
- What venue would you choose?
- How would you and your partner design the invitations?
- What kind of rings would you and your mate desire?
- What kind of accommodations would you have for your guests?
- What would be the menu for the receptions?
- What singer, band, performer, or DJ would be the entertainment?
- Who would be on your fantasy guest list?
- Who would design the tuxedo, wedding gown, and wedding party garments?
- Who would design the rings, and how much would they cost?
- What would be the budget?
- Who would be the photographer, videographer, and planner?

Planning Notes:

Who can provide "expert" knowledge, if necessary?

_____

_____

What items do you need to bring?

_____

_____

Where will the activity take place?

_____

_____

When will the activity take place?

_____

_____

Additional Pre-activity Notes:

_____

_____

Post-Activity Notes, Ideas, & Suggestions:

_____

_____

_____

_____

_____

_____

_____

_____

_____

_____

_____

_____

Activity No. 45: Fantasy Shopping Spree

You can do this activity by shopping online together or making a trip to a mall. The goal isn't to make actual purchases but to familiarize yourself with some of the most coveted brands on the market. Don't be satisfied with what influencers claim is the best, nor should you be strong-armed by advertisers. Don't fall into rank with "stans" and mindlessly copy-cat celebrities. Don't be a status-seeker, symbol-slave, or logo-lover.

Research the brands. Read their labels and fine print. Know the history of the designers and the motivation behind the designs. Attempt to touch, feel, sample, try, rent, examine, smell, and know personally before making any claims, decisions, or commitments. Keep in mind that a brand's customer appreciation, quality assurance, and customer service are just as important as the products it offers.

Experience for yourself! Place a premium on quality—nothing else—and dare to dream outside your comfort zone. What you envision today and dream about tonight just might become your reality tomorrow! Share a grand fantasy with your partner—the two of you are the united force that could make it happen!

Planning Notes:

Who can provide "expert" knowledge, if necessary?

_____

_____

What items do you need to bring?

_____

_____

Where will the activity take place?

_____

_____

When will the activity take place?

_____

_____

Additional Pre-activity Notes:

_____

_____

Post-Activity Notes, Ideas, & Suggestions:

Activity No. 46: Museums "R" Us

From the comfort of your sofa or your cozy comforter, you two can virtually tour some of the most astonishing art collections at the world's most renowned museums. Get out the wine glasses, the charcuterie board, the vegetable tray, the fruit basket, the chocolate mousse, the crème brûlée, and the Catena Zapata. Spray the area with a little essence of rose, lavender, or lemon, and set the playlist to some jazz, with a little classical sprinkled here and there. Set up your television or laptop for viewing and get the show on the road.

New York offers some of the best virtual visits: the Guggenheim with its famed Frank Lloyd Wright rotunda; the Metropolitan Museum of Art and its impressive collection; the Museum of Modern Art and its 129 masterpieces, including Van Gogh's Starry Night, and Cézanne's Still Life with Apples; the Whitney Museum; and the American Museum of Natural History, with more than 2200 objects to swoon over in its virtual collection.

Peruse the collections of museums all over the world:

The National Gallery of Art in Washington D.C. has two virtual exhibits. One is a fashion exhibit, and the other is an art exhibit.

The Van Gogh Museum in Amsterdam, the Netherlands, is an amazing homage to the artist which houses 750 personal letters, 500 sketches/drawings, and 200 paintings.

The Pergamon Museum in Berlin is a historical museum that

boasts of several ancient artifacts, including the Pergamon Altar and the Ishtar Gate of Babylon.

The Musée du Louvre, one of the most famous museums in all the world, is located in Paris.

The Musée d'Orsay, which offers a virtual walkthrough of works from Cézanne, Gauguin, Monet, and many others.

The National Museum of Anthropology in Mexico City has an extensive virtual offering that includes ancient artifacts from the Mayan civilization.

The British Museum of London with a virtual visit that includes the Great Court, The Rosetta Stone, and Egyptian Mummies.

You and your lover have several options to choose from, so enjoy the day at the museum cuddling together in your birthday suits!

Planning Notes:

Who can provide "expert" knowledge, if necessary?

_____

_____

What items do you need to bring?

_____

_____

Where will the activity take place?

_____

_____

When will the activity take place?

_____

_____

Additional Pre-activity Notes:

_____

_____

Post-Activity Notes, Ideas, & Suggestions:

_____

_____

_____

_____

_____

_____

_____

_____

_____

_____

_____

_____

_____

Activity No. 47: Ride with Me!

A Luxury Ride

Everyone has a dream ride: well, *almost* everyone. What's your dream ride? What is your mate's? Consider renting your favorite rides for a day, a weekend, or a week. Jet around town, take a long drive together, go on a few fun outings. Catch a sunrise or watch a sunset. Enjoy the luxury—enjoy the ride! Do it all behind the wheel of a luxury automobile!

A Horseback Ride

Horseback riding is both serene and adventurous. Whether you're watching the sunrise or sunset, catching some sun rays, smelling the sweet aroma of wildflowers wafting in the air, galloping through pastures, trail riding along a beach coastline, stopping to rub your horse's neck or side and looking out over a mountain range, or trotting through the countryside, being outdoors with your love on horseback can take your breath away.

If you are not experienced riders, it might be helpful to have that third experienced person "tagging" along with you. You could also choose to "tag along" with an experienced couple or team for extra safety; in this case, the more the merrier! You can take a quick break to view a picturesque scene, find a place to enjoy a light lunch, or even mimic the old Western films and set up a campfire at dusk, roasting marshmallows and telling stories to the group. There are so many different ways to enjoy a horseback ride...just remember to softly whisper a few loving words in your sweetie's ear and plant a few kisses on your sweetie's lips!

A Bike Ride

If you and your *mon cher* own bikes, get them out and plan a bike ride together! Find a trail that you've never ridden together and stop along the trail to kiss, frolic, and fondle. If you don't own bikes, many parks, trails, and areas throughout most cities have easy bike rental stands or establishments. You can then take a ride through a beautiful park, along a trail that's nestled against a winding stream, around a city that you have never seen before, or just throughout your local neighborhood. No matter where you choose to ride, take breaks along the way to kiss, frolic, and fondle!

A Camel Ride

If you and your honey bunny are in a desert region of the world—like Egypt, Morocco, or wherever camel riding is possible—you need to make this happen. Many tourist spots like Australia, China, and Dubai offer unique camelback riding treks. If you and your baby-cakes visit any of the aforementioned, I encourage you to take a ride together. Plan the excursion so that it can be as romantic as possible: try to schedule it as the sun is going down and as the day is cooling. If possible, hire a guide to arrange a romantic fire pit meal under the stars and take you through a wildlife reserve to see indigenous animals in their natural habitat. You might be able to trek along lakes, ocean shores, and through mountainous regions. Whatever you do, take the romance to the limit and enjoy!

A Motorcycle, Motorbike, or Moped Ride

This is not an adventure for the novice or the inexperienced, and you should wear a helmet and proper clothing at all times. If you and your partner can enjoy a ride together safely, this is an exciting way to explore a new city. When traveling abroad, you can rent a motorcycle in a country like Italy, where some of the most beautiful city streets are narrow and winding, making it a popular transportation choice for locals. It can be an adventurous way to explore the countryside, a state park, or a quaint beach community. Have fun, and most importantly—be safe!

Planning Notes:

Who can provide "expert" knowledge, if necessary?

_____

_____

What items do you need to bring?

_____

_____

Where will the activity take place?

_____

_____

When will the activity take place?

_____

_____

Additional Pre-activity Notes:

_____

_____

Post-Activity Notes, Ideas, & Suggestions:

_____

_____

_____

_____

_____

_____

_____

_____

_____

_____

_____

_____

_____

ਤੁਸੀਂ ਮੇਰੀ ਜ਼ਿੰਦਗੀ ਦਾ
ਪਹਿਸਾਰ ਹੋ

Activity No. 48: Make Me Over

Every now and then, we can all use a style overhaul. It's easy to get stuck in a routine (that should actually be called a rut) and keep doing what we've always done. Maybe our mate has become accustomed to our appearance, but we aren't putting in quite the same amount of effort that we once did. Perhaps, we were never really stylish, but to demonstrate our devotion to our partners, we are willing to try a new look. Maybe you both want to level up and improve your appearance. Or, if we do have style and our mate would like to see us in a different look, then be open—this change is not permanent.

To complete your makeover, try hiring a trusted stylist to shop with you and your partner for an entire day. A good stylist can recommend styles and brands that are suited for your body type, budget, and taste. Perhaps, you want to go from business suits to cool, contemporary casual, or from the mundane work uniform to eye-catching denim wear. Maybe you want your mate to move past those flip flops and faded tees to a more form-fitting physique that shows some style. Whatever the case, both of you should be willing to go to a new level.

Once you have worked with a clothing stylist, consider a new hairstyle, cut, and/or color, and consult a professional hairstylist that specializes in what you and your partner desire. Do not penny-pinch; in most cases, you will get what you pay for, and this is not the time to take that gamble. Your aim is to please both yourself and your mate with your new look. If you wear makeup, need to learn new techniques, or would like to enhance your beauty, locate a trusted makeup artist or visit your local Ulta, Sephora, or Mac stores, and request a consultation and makeover. Choose a look that you can maintain, and don't be afraid to check out YouTube for useful tutorials. Below are just a few ideas that you and your SST (Sweet Sexy Thing) may incorporate:

- New Eyeglasses or Lasik Eye surgery
- Teeth Whitening
- Dental Work
- Specialized Facial Treatment(s)
- Hair Cut or Color
- Eyebrow shaping
- Lash Extensions
- Body Waxing
- Manicure and Pedicure
- Moustache and/or Beard grooming
- New sneakers, boots, loafers, flip flops—just discard whatever is old, outdated, and worn.
- New clothing
- Makeup Makeover

Tips to Remember:

Keep it fun! Look for ways to incorporate needed changes and be willing to keep up the work to look your best for yourself. Stay committed to the progress and keep working until you uncover the best version of yourself for you and your mate. Be versatile—you might require ongoing assistance so that you can be appropriately styled for your lifestyle. Athletic, business, casual, outdoor, and formal are all clothing categories, and you may need help in one or more areas. You may love change going from urban wear to formal wear to rodeo wear—do it ALL! Just do it well and do it in style. As they say, represent! Make sure to take before and after photos. Do a couple's photoshoot!

Planning Notes:

Who can provide "expert" knowledge, if necessary?

_____

_____

What items do you need to bring?

_____

_____

Where will the activity take place?

_____

_____

When will the activity take place?

_____

_____

Additional Pre-activity Notes:

_____

_____

Post–Activity Notes, Ideas, & Suggestions:

_____

_____

_____

_____

_____

_____

_____

_____

_____

_____

_____

_____

_____

_____

Activity No. 49: Stand by Me, Stanza by Stanza

Pull out a fresh note pad, pens, dictionary, thesaurus, rhyming dictionary, and a book of poems as a guide. Set the stage by wearing only robes and your birthday suits! Have your favorite snacks prepared, whether morning, midday, or evening. You and your partner are going to go stanza-by-stanza and write romantic poems together. They can be serious, funny, or witty. The key is to bond and have fun.

One of you can start with the first line. If you need inspiration, ask your partner to disrobe, or you can flip through the thesaurus and dictionaries for words that catch your attention. You and your partner should take turns until you feel that your poem is complete. When you have completed your poem, you can disrobe and read it together, side by side. This is the time to hug, kiss, caress, laugh, and just enjoy one another. Try it again and again; you'll be amazed at what you two come up with. If you decide to write and recite to one each other, disrobe, face one another, and get as close as possible!

Planning Notes:

Who can provide "expert" knowledge, if necessary?

_____

_____

What items do you need to bring?

_____

_____

Where will the activity take place?

_____

_____

When will the activity take place?

_____

_____

Additional Pre-activity Notes:

_____

_____

Post-Activity Notes, Ideas, & Suggestions:

Activity No. 50: Paint and Play

Gather those painting supplies. When choosing your canvas, remember that both acrylic and watercolor paints dry easily. You may choose an actual canvas, some denim jeans, a denim jacket, or an old sheet. Whatever you like will work. The point is to just be free and creative in the presence of the one you love.

You both should determine the rules: you can use fingers, body parts, brushes, sponges, stencils—it doesn't matter. Visit YouTube for ideas and instructional videos. Just find and prepare a proper place to paint so you do not ruin your belongings. If you can, try to borrow or rent space from another painter. Experiment, experience, and enjoy!

When you're finished, enjoy a bath or shower ritual together. Allow your work of art to dry, then find a home for it. Maybe the two of you will decide to make a collection!

Planning Notes:

Who can provide "expert" knowledge, if necessary?

_____

_____

What items do you need to bring?

_____

_____

Where will the activity take place?

_____

_____

When will the activity take place?

_____

_____

Additional Pre-activity Notes:

_____

_____

Post–Activity Notes, Ideas, & Suggestions:

Activity No. 51: Fantasy Photoshoot

Would you be daring enough to don a Marvel character's costume, cosplay as a game or anime character, in full body paint to look like an avatar, or anything else that catches your fancy? It can be both refreshing and encouraging just to see ourselves differently, which can also allow our mates to see us in a whole new way. In our loved one's life, we might be a figurative superhero or heroine to them, and vice versa. However, seeing each other in costume will bring to life what we mean to each other, and it is a reminder of how much we cherish each other for the roles we play in one another's lives. A fantasy photoshoot can be a fun way to show each other of how much we are appreciated.

Perhaps your mate comes from a lineage that they would like to honor, whether it be Indigenous Americans, Texas Cowboys, Spanish Flamenco dancers, or an overlooked and undervalued group. Having your mate celebrate their heritage in this way could allow them to pay homage to their ancestry and culture. These fantasy photos have no limitations or restrictions except to your imagination. Clothing and costumes can be rented, borrowed, handmade, or pieced together by going to thrift stores and resale shops. Be creative. You can hire photographers, or take the photos yourself. It is amazing how well some of the cameras on mobile phones operate, and it is unbelievable how many apps are available for download to your mobile phone for editing photos. In any case, snap away!

Nudie Photo Shoot

Would you be comfortable, daring, and free enough to do a tastefully risqué photoshoot with a respected and reputable photographer with your partner? Would you be comfortable, daring, and willing to do a tastefully risqué photoshoot with you and/or your partner behind the camera instead?

Remember that if you do choose to go with an outside photographer, you do not want your photographs in the possession of any party who is not responsible enough to protect your privacy, bottom-line.

If you feel confident and safe enough to join in a phot-op this racy, it can be a wonderful experience capturing the beauty of you and your partner. These images are particularly beautiful when a woman is pregnant.

To prepare for the shoot, go prop shopping in advance. Furs—both faux and authentic—are always fun. Bold jewelry pieces can make a statement on bare skin. Accessories of all sorts can add flair, humor and a stylish twist—think scarves, hats, gloves, heels, boots, etc. Body makeup may help you and/or your partner feel more at ease; you can also consider airbrushing, spray tanning, body paint, body glitter, and any other ways to adorn or "perfect" the appearance of the complexion. Because you will want to present your best, consider a fresh haircut, beard trim, hair coloring, hairstyle, pedicure and/or manicure, or any beauty service that will ensure you look and feel your best.

Set the stage. Organize all the props and accessories. Hire an on-site stylist and makeup artist, if feasible. You can hire them if you're working in a studio with a photographer or if you're working from home. However, if you choose to shoot in your own abode, confirm that all outside parties are comfortable working in your home for a risqué photoshoot. Some artists may not be comfortable, so ask these questions before booking them. Have ample refreshments, wipes, towels, seating, lighting, and tables available for prepping.

Establish the Tone. If it is all frolic and fun, then make sure to have an upbeat playlist and fun refreshments and drinks. You do not want anything too serious. If you want to establish a serene mood, try playing nature sounds, crafting good teas and coffee, and lighting aromatherapy candles. You can massage one another between shots. If you are wanting to evoke an artistic mood, you may try a little classical and jazz with a cognac and champagne bar.

Provide an assortment of coffee table books that feature photography, art, architecture, and/or music. For the lover in you, play songs that incite amorous feelings between you and your mate, and bring out the wine, chocolates, and roses. In between shots, hug, kiss, caress, cuddle, and cajole. If you or your lover are the sassy "throwback" types, then prepare some naughty cocktails like Sex on the Beach, Leg Spreader, Climax, Forbidden Fruit, Between the Sheets, Screamin' Orgasm, Angel's Tit, Blow Job, and Slippery Nipple, to name a few. In this mood, you and your mate might enjoy a little disco music. Have fun and do a little dirty dancing in between shots and photo shots! If you're that western duo, then you had better have a little country music, some beers, good whisky, perhaps a Naughty Cowgirl cocktail, and do a little two-stepping in between. For the health enthusiasts, set the mood with fresh juices on ice, a smoothie bar, and an eclectic music assortment, include some good house, ska, reggae, and global beats. You may also enjoy stretching in between shots and taking photos doing yoga poses.

If this is all new to you, well bring on the sparkling water, have a playlist of TEDTalks, turn on NPR's Tiny Desk, and enjoy. Whatever works for you and your partner, bring it!

Monitor the Mood. Always make sure that your partner and anyone else present is comfortable and enjoying themselves. Ask, observe, and seek input.

Planning Notes:

Who can provide "expert" knowledge, if necessary?

_____

_____

What items do you need to bring?

_____

_____

Where will the activity take place?

_____

_____

When will the activity take place?

_____

_____

Additional Pre-activity Notes:

_____

_____

Post-Activity Notes, Ideas, & Suggestions:

_____

_____

_____

_____

_____

_____

_____

_____

_____

_____

_____

_____

_____

שְׁנֵי שָׁדַיִךְ כִּשְׁנֵי עֲפָרִים,
תְּאֳמֵי צְבִיָּה.

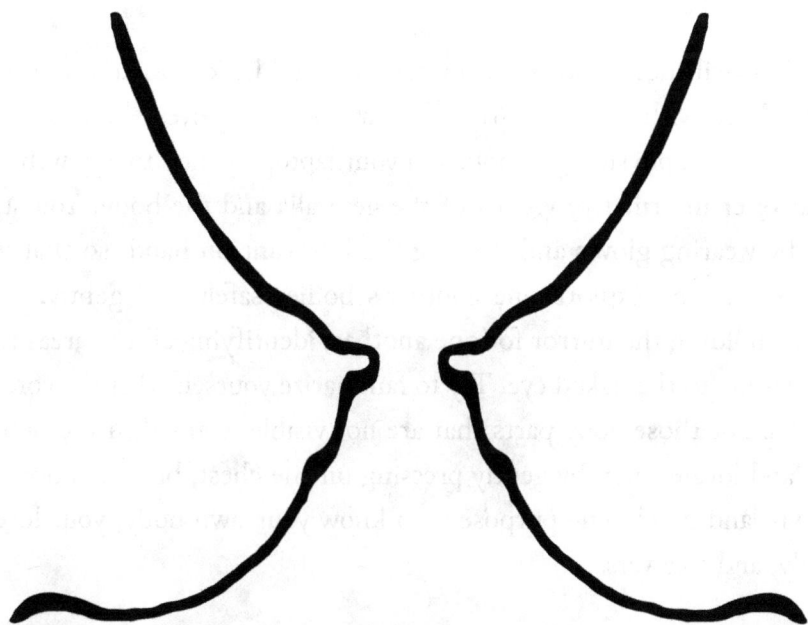

Activity No. 52: Doctor, Doctor

How well do you know your anatomy and that of your partner? How well do you think your partner knows his/her own and your anatomy? Well, just as I have advised over and over again, get ready to set the stage, establish the tone, and monitor the mood.

You will need two hand mirrors, a nice blanket, a large towel or soft sheet with enough space for two, sterile gloves, lubricant, an anatomy and physiology book, and your laptop opened to any websites that offer informative visuals of the genitalia and the body. You start off by wearing gloves and keeping the lubricant on hand, so that you can touch and explore one another's bodies safely and gently. Take turns holding the mirror for one another, identifying all the areas that are visible to the naked eye. Try to familiarize yourself with the correct terms. For those body parts that are not visible, you will use touch to try and locate them by gently pressing on the chest, breast, abdomen, pelvis, and navel. The purpose is to know your own body, your lover's body, and vice versa.

Scour the pages of the anatomy books. Watch informative YouTube videos, and view as many diagrams as possible. Understanding each other's bodies can help you both stay healthy, as you may be able to detect breast lumps that could be malignant, rectal fissures that could lead to future issues, infections that could be contagious, and the start of hemorrhoids that could be very painful. Being comfortable with and knowledgeable of your own and each other's bodies is important for a healthy love life.

Planning Notes:

Who can provide "expert" knowledge, if necessary?

_____

_____

What items do you need to bring?

_____

_____

Where will the activity take place?

_____

_____

When will the activity take place?

_____

_____

Additional Pre-activity Notes:

_____

_____

Post-Activity Notes, Ideas, & Suggestions:

_____

_____

_____

_____

_____

_____

_____

_____

_____

_____

_____

_____

_____

Activity No. 53: Donate Date

Sometimes, the best way to show our mate our capacity to care is by demonstrating love and concern for others—strangers included. Invite your mate to join you in donating time, resources, and/or funds to a worthy cause, whether it be a shelter or someone in need. Determine what you are going to do beforehand, then do it together. If the two of you can make a habit of being kind, considerate, and charitable toward strangers, how much easier should it be for you to be so toward one another?

Planning Notes:

Who can provide "expert" knowledge, if necessary?

_____

What items do you need to bring?

_____

_____

Where will the activity take place?

_____

_____

When will the activity take place?

_____

_____

Additional Pre-activity Notes:

_____

_____

Post-Activity Notes, Ideas, & Suggestions:

_____

_____

_____

_____

_____

_____

_____

_____

_____

_____

_____

_____

_____

Activity No. 54: Volunteer on Valentine's

Typically, Valentine's Day is the day for lovers to commemorate their love for each other. However, what if you and your lover joined efforts and decided to show love to the less fortunate? Locate a local shelter or non-profit agency that could benefit from your volunteering for the day. You and your sweetheart could decide to create your own way of showing consideration for others. You could take roses and candy to a women's shelter; bring flowers and small stuffed animals to an elderly citizens' home; visit a ward of the Children's hospital with toys, books, and games; deliver donuts to another group of volunteers; or pass out books, balls, and trinkets to parents with small children at a local park in an at-risk community.

After you and your sweetheart have completed your acts of kindness, make sure to deliver a treat to your sweetheart in their primary love language. Your sweetheart might appreciate a card with a heartfelt handwritten sentiment affirming your love, or maybe all you want is more quality time. Perhaps, your sweetheart would appreciate you taking the vehicle for service, detailing, and fueling, and you might be ecstatic to receive those new golf clubs you had been eyeing. Could it be that more than anything, you both would love to be in each other's arms cuddling, caressing, and kissing?

Planning Notes:

Who can provide "expert" knowledge, if necessary?

_____

_____

What items do you need to bring?

_____

_____

Where will the activity take place?

_____

_____

When will the activity take place?

_____

_____

Additional Pre-activity Notes:

_____

_____

Post-Activity Notes, Ideas, & Suggestions:

_____

_____

_____

_____

_____

_____

_____

_____

_____

_____

_____

_____

Activity No. 55: Pay it Backward for a Day

Maybe you've heard of "Paying it Forward," the concept of doing something kind for someone else and asking them to extend that action to another person, and so on. This concept is the same. Choose a day when you and your sugar are out and about and running errands. Each time you make a purchase, you two can tell the cashier that you'll be paying for the items of the person in line behind you. If and when the recipient acknowledges the gesture, you can ask them to do the same "sometime down the line."

After a day of giving, talk with your mate about how it made you both feel. You know the rule: make one another feel loved!

Planning Notes:

Who can provide "expert" knowledge, if necessary?

_____

_____

What items do you need to bring?

_____

_____

Where will the activity take place?

_____

_____

When will the activity take place?

_____

_____

Additional Pre-activity Notes:

_____

_____

Post-Activity Notes, Ideas, & Suggestions:

Activity No. 56: Plan a Couple's Dinner

Think about hosting a couple for dinner. By now, you both should be familiar with setting the stage, establishing the tone, and monitoring the mood. Decide on a menu and if it will be purchased from a restaurant and set up at your home, catered by a catering company, or made by you and your partner. Make sure that you have those sexy cocktails and naughty chocolates available. Plan activities for the evening, and consider adding some of the "sexy" board games that every attendee can play. Play charades, card games, and any other games that couples would enjoy. Hire a masseuse to come and teach a couple's massage class, or a yoga instructor to show couples how to help each other stretch. You and your mate could teach your friends how to make their own naughty chocolates, edible body paint, and massage oils. Hand out goodie bags that will inspire them to create future romantic moments.

After the dinner, discuss with your partner how hosting a romantic dinner for other couples made them feel. Discuss it during one of your romantic bathing rituals, and let that be the reward for the hard work.

Go all out and get it all in!

Planning Notes:

Who can provide "expert" knowledge, if necessary?

_____

_____

What items do you need to bring?

_____

_____

Where will the activity take place?

_____

_____

When will the activity take place?

_____

_____

Additional Pre-activity Notes:

_____

_____

Post–Activity Notes, Ideas, & Suggestions:

Activity No. 57: Naked Car Wash

I hope you have a backyard with a water hose that offers you both the space and privacy to enjoy washing your vehicles butt-naked! If you have the water hose and space, but not the privacy, then wear something sexy yet minimal: a tee with no bra, a teeny-weeny bikini, some skimpy shorts, etc. The goal is to get the vehicles clean while you and your lover get down and dirty! Clean the interiors first so that when the two of you start cleaning the exteriors, you can get wet and soapy. That is where the loving begins: rub, bump, slide, glide, hug, kiss, caress, and canoodle.

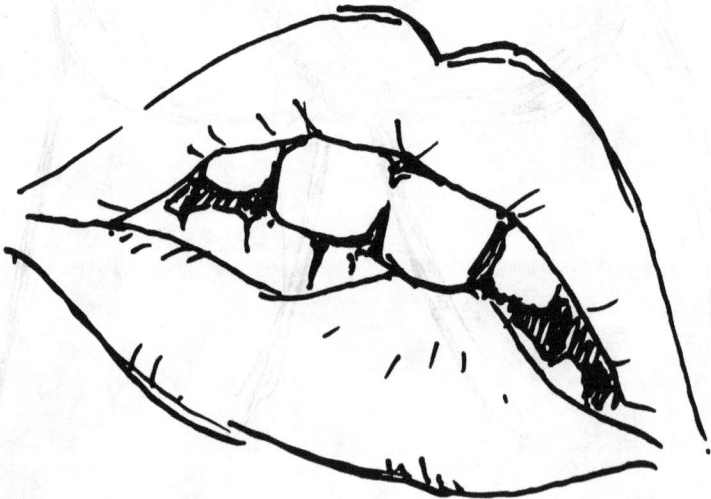

Planning Notes:

Who can provide "expert" knowledge, if necessary?

_____

_____

What items do you need to bring?

_____

_____

Where will the activity take place?

_____

_____

When will the activity take place?

_____

_____

Additional Pre-activity Notes:

_____

_____

Post–Activity Notes, Ideas, & Suggestions:

Activity No. 58: Host Your Private Toy Party

You can find a company like Lovewinx that hosts adult toy parties if you want to share this fun with other couples you know. If you just want to have your own little private party, you can find adult toy stores online. You don't have to make any purchase quite yet, since your goal is to discuss and explore future possibilities. Make your party everything that you and your lover desire it to be.

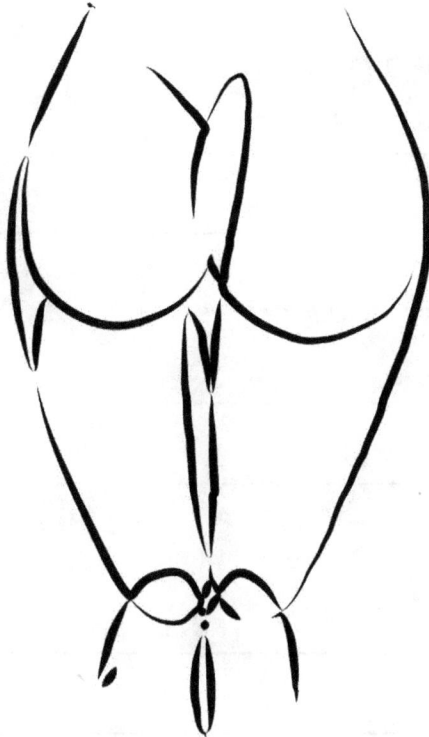

Planning Notes:

Who can provide "expert" knowledge, if necessary?

_____

_____

What items do you need to bring?

_____

_____

Where will the activity take place?

_____

_____

When will the activity take place?

_____

_____

Additional Pre-activity Notes:

_____

_____

Post-Activity Notes, Ideas, & Suggestions:

_____

_____

_____

_____

_____

_____

_____

_____

_____

_____

_____

_____

_____

Activity No. 59: Train for a Walk, Run, or Marathon Together

You might be fortunate enough to have a physically fit mate, though ideally, you both are. Maybe you are fit, but your mate isn't quite at your level. Maybe neither of you have ever been fit and want to get into shape for the first time, or you both were once very fit, but need to get back in "the saddle." It doesn't matter either way: the only thing that counts is that you both agree to work together, go the distance, and be patient with one another.

If one or both of you is experienced, then develop a customized and foolproof plan to get back into shape. If neither of you is experienced, you can join a club in your community, hire an experienced trainer, or seek online instruction. Invest in proper gear (you can match if you like), focus on safety and injury prevention, and learn stretching techniques, proper ways to fuel your bodies, and strategies for success. Sooner or later, you'll find yourselves looking forward to the time you spend training together. This activity may be the precursor for many other activities that you enjoy together, like your shower, bathing, hair grooming, massage, laundry, or Chick Flick/RomCom rituals.

Planning Notes:

Who can provide "expert" knowledge, if necessary?

_____

_____

What items do you need to bring?

_____

_____

Where will the activity take place?

_____

_____

When will the activity take place?

_____

_____

Additional Pre-activity Notes:

_____

_____

Post-Activity Notes, Ideas, & Suggestions:

Activity No. 60: Learn a Couple's Dance

Nothing is more elegant, sensual, and romantic than couples dancing. It is a splendid way to get in a little cardio while also being able to caress your partner. There are so many styles of dance. If you want to learn a little Latin sizzle, then you and your partner may opt to learn Salsa, Rumba, Tango, Meringue, Bachata, Bolero, Cha-Cha, Samba, or Paso Doble. If you want to dance American style, you can try East Coast or West Coast Swing, Two-Step, the Quick-Step, or Chicago Step. You and your partner may want to opt for more traditional styles, like the Waltz, Fox Trot, or Foxatino. Whichever dance you choose, try to commit to at least one weekly lesson.

Invest in proper ballroom dance shoes, because they will help you develop proper technique. Don't wait to purchase the proper shoes after several lessons have already passed; it will make your learning experience even more challenging. I think you will find this to be a rewarding endeavor for you and your partner—just remember to be patient!

Planning Notes:

Who can provide "expert" knowledge, if necessary?

_____

_____

What items do you need to bring?

_____

_____

Where will the activity take place?

_____

_____

When will the activity take place?

_____

_____

Additional Pre-activity Notes:

_____

_____

Post-Activity Notes, Ideas, & Suggestions:

Activity No. 61: James Bond It

For a fun, explosive weekend, you and your secret agent can enjoy firearms training, race car driving lessons, self-defense classes, and a pepper ball gun demonstration. Before you take the courses, watch a few James Bond flicks to get in the groove.

Purchase some cool, black, "secret agent" garb: sleek, stretchy commuter slacks, fitted sweaters, sleek leather jackets, black militia sets, and SWAT team-like attire are all options that can make you and your lover feel "legit." Dress the part and play the roles for the weekend. Enjoy action films with your mate, make sexy cocktails, meet each other dressed as secret agents in fancy hotel lobbies, and have a few cocktails or glasses of wine at their bars. Take the fun back to the house, have a few nightcaps, and make out with your secret agent!

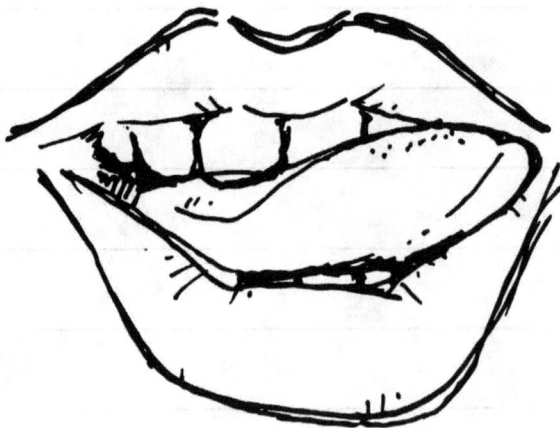

Planning Notes:

Who can provide "expert" knowledge, if necessary?

_____

_____

What items do you need to bring?

_____

_____

Where will the activity take place?

_____

_____

When will the activity take place?

_____

_____

Additional Pre-activity Notes:

_____

_____

Post-Activity Notes, Ideas, & Suggestions:

Activity No. 62: Build, Create, or Shop for Your Castle

This is a fun exercise that can be accomplished under the sheets with your lover and your laptop. There are programs online that help you build your dream home in 3D. You can visit *www.planner5d.com* and home.by.me, or surf the net for other free online options. There are several mobile apps available to assist you and your honey as well, and they range from floor plan design to color palette selections, and flooring to furnishing. This is a fun and interactive way to discover what you and your partner prefer.

If you do not own a home, then this will teach you about the challenges you may face and compromises you may have to make when considering a home purchase. In this case, you can begin working on them as soon as possible. If you already own a home, this may encourage new hopes, dreams, aspirations, and goals. If you are pleased and have no desire for a dream home, perhaps it can be a tool for you and your partner should you want to redecorate, remodel, or renovate your current dwelling. If you are thinking about buying a home in the near future, tools such as this can help you and your mate determine your desires and needs. This is a good starting point, and if nothing else, it is an exciting interactive adult game to enjoy in the convenience of your cozy bed. You and your partner can make this exercise as eventful and as meaningful as you two desire.

Planning Notes:

Who can provide "expert" knowledge, if necessary?

_____

_____

What items do you need to bring?

_____

_____

Where will the activity take place?

_____

_____

When will the activity take place?

_____

_____

Additional Pre-activity Notes:

_____

_____

Post-Activity Notes, Ideas, & Suggestions:

_____

_____

_____

_____

_____

_____

_____

_____

_____

_____

_____

_____

情人眼里出西施

Activity No. 63: Pole Dance and Strip Tease, Please!

I believe that pole dancing and strip teasing is a sexy and loving gesture when done for your lover and your lover, only. You and your partner may locate a studio with instructors that can teach you and your partner techniques privately. You may learn enough from one class to impress your mate at home anytime you want to give a little show. Just be willing to invest in the necessary equipment and attire for staging your private performance.

You and/or your lover might enjoy the initial class so much that you'll want to continue taking private lessons. If nothing else, it's a great work out, and one that you will be able to do in the privacy of your home for your one and only!

Planning Notes:

Who can provide "expert" knowledge, if necessary?

_____

_____

What items do you need to bring?

_____

_____

Where will the activity take place?

_____

_____

When will the activity take place?

_____

_____

Additional Pre-activity Notes:

_____

_____

Post-Activity Notes, Ideas, & Suggestions:

_____

_____

_____

_____

_____

_____

_____

_____

_____

_____

_____

_____

_____

Activity No. 64: A Servant's Heart

Every now and then, whether you or your mate admit it, you both could use a day of "unconditional, no questions asked, just anticipate my needs" kind of support. It's such a selfless gift to give to a deserving companion, and it takes a servant's heart to be able to serve in this capacity.

For example, you know that your mate has a huge project and business trip coming up that requires total focus. As a result, you with your heart to serve will have your partner's meals prepared; pick up the dry cleaning needed for the trip; go to the Apple store to replace the headsets that your love lost; run to the bank to complete a wire transfer that has to be done before they leave; cancel the credit card that they accidentally lost and make arrangements for your love to have funds; handle the appointment with the technician who is repairing the Smart TV; pack their luggage for the business trip, etc. Your partner might have been impatient, curt, and demanding as the pressure to complete the project is mounting, so you take it all in stride—this is just one of those days that you know that you're needed. You realize that days like this are few and far between, and your partner needs you more than ever to have a servant's heart.

Conversely, you've just found out that you'll need to have surgery on your reproductive organs. You're upset because you were just promoted and don't want to take time off, even though you have sick leave. Your partner has decided to take leave so that you can have the support you need to work from home. Your partner has agreed to do all house cleaning, meal prepping, clothes laundering, running all errands, and to do them exactly as you wish. You are meticulous, and your partner realizes that the critiques and corrections are just a part of it all. Your partner, without voicing one complaint, does and redoes the house cleaning; cooks and recooks the salmon, the brown rice, the kale, the parsnips; folds and refolds the laundry so that it fits perfectly in their designated drawers; goes to the market several times per day because what was purchased was not exactly what you requested. Your partner knows that you're in pain, that moodiness and short temper are not typical, and that you're trying to work through it. Your partner has a servant's heart and just wants to get through this and back to the loving side.

By the end of it all, you both have perfected meeting and anticipating each other's needs, and you are now closer than ever.

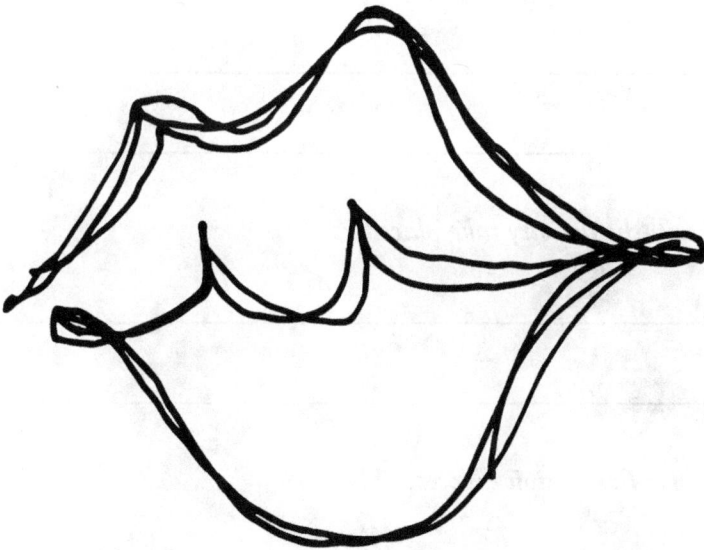

Planning Notes:

Who can provide "expert" knowledge, if necessary?

_____

_____

What items do you need to bring?

_____

_____

Where will the activity take place?

_____

_____

When will the activity take place?

_____

_____

Additional Pre-activity Notes:

_____

_____

Post–Activity Notes, Ideas, & Suggestions:

_____

_____

_____

_____

_____

_____

_____

_____

_____

_____

_____

_____

Activity No. 65: Poems for My Love

Collect a series of poems dedicated to your lover and have your lover do the same. You can write them by hand, have a calligrapher script them, or print them from sites online. Make sure to give proper credit to the poets and be sure that you have permission to copy and reprint them.

Collect the pages, find a craft supply store like MJ Designs, Michael's, Hobby Lobby, or Joann's, and purchase a scrapbook so that you and your love can create a customized book of poems together. Don't forget to grab some permanent markers, stickers, and other tools that are recommended for scrap-booking. You can visit *www.scrapbook.com* to shop for items or to inquire about classes for making your scrapbook.

Prepare your play space at home. Get the coffee pot brewing, the wine glasses ready, the cheese and crackers on a tray, and find the playlist you and your love think would put you both in a creative amorous mood. Spend the evening making your book together, sipping on your favorite wine, singing with your playlist, and reading your selected poems to each other.

Planning Notes:

Who can provide "expert" knowledge, if necessary?

_____

_____

What items do you need to bring?

_____

_____

Where will the activity take place?

_____

_____

When will the activity take place?

_____

_____

Additional Pre-activity Notes:

_____

_____

Post–Activity Notes, Ideas, & Suggestions:

Activity No. 66: Teatime

"Teatime" is always a wonderful way to share quality time with your partner. Hot tea on a cold winter day, when you or your bae have the body ache blues, to heal and invigorate the body, or with a little rum for a nighttime elixir are all ways that hot tea can be appreciated. However, let's not forget the importance of old fashioned iced tea. This cool beverage can be so refreshing on a hot summer day by the pool, after a long run or strenuous workout, as a night time refresher, or when spiked with a little rum, tequila, gin, or vodka for that Long Island getaway right at home. For both you and your lover's pleasure, enjoy your teatime together.

You can visit your local herbal shop, go online to find an assortment of tea blends, or you can order individual herbs, dried flowers, spices, and other essences to make your own blends. Always invest in the best ingredients for the best flavor. Pick out a tea set with dainty cups and/or manly mugs that will make you and your love want to just sit around and sip some tea. You can find a teapot, tea set, teacups, and mugs at local department stores, cool vintage shops, or online. Ceramic, porcelain, stainless steel, iron, silver-plated, sterling silver, glass—these are just a few of the different materials that you can find your perfect mug or pitcher in!

There is a myriad of items that you can use to make your teatime delightful. Familiarize yourselves with the different strainers, tea makers, tea selections, loose leaf tea diffusers, luxury teapots, blooming teas, wellness teas, electric tea warmers, electric tea kettles, self-steeping tea mugs, and any other items made for tea. You may want to invest in a tea tray or cart to stash all of your tea-related items in. You two lovebirds can purchase whatever you like: the key is to set aside time to take your tea.

Maybe you can decide to speak the "t" (truth) over tea. This can be a time when you agree to come together amicably to discuss important matters. You can set the stage with your fully stocked portable tea cart, and make sure that you have all the additions you both enjoy—special kinds of honey, sweeteners, lemon wedges, fresh herbs, or whatever else you want. Get comfy on the sofa, take the cart bedside and set up tea on your tea tray, sit face to face at your dining room table, or take it to the office where you can have access to your computers. Establish a tone that will be conducive for open communication, and monitor the mood—keep the tea flowing, the conversation going, and most of all...the love flowing!

Planning Notes:

Who can provide "expert" knowledge, if necessary?

_____

_____

What items do you need to bring?

_____

_____

Where will the activity take place?

_____

_____

When will the activity take place?

_____

_____

Additional Pre-activity Notes:

_____

_____

Post-Activity Notes, Ideas, & Suggestions:

_____

_____

_____

_____

_____

_____

_____

_____

_____

_____

_____

_____

_____

Activity No. 67: Tee Time

Another beautiful way to bond with your partner is on a golf outing. Golf courses often feature some of the most beautiful terrains in the area with their well-maintained foliage and well-manicured greens. If neither of you golf, take private lessons together. If one or both of you golf, get a cart and load it with golf course approved beverages and snacks, and enjoy the outdoors, the scenery, and the game.

Every once in a while, help your partner or pretend to help them by standing behind and pressing against them while you offer instruction on their swing technique. Check YouTube for examples if you need to. It's a great way to sneak in a little "bump and grind" unsuspected, out in broad daylight, while on the green!

Planning Notes:

Who can provide "expert" knowledge, if necessary?

_____

_____

What items do you need to bring?

_____

_____

Where will the activity take place?

_____

_____

When will the activity take place?

_____

_____

Additional Pre-activity Notes:

_____

_____

Post-Activity Notes, Ideas, & Suggestions:

Activity No. 68: Snowed Out

For those of us in climates that don't experience snow that often, a day in the snow is always a winter wonderland. If you live in an area where it snows often, it can still be a treat to go visit the nearest ski resort for a mini-vacay. You can enjoy skiing, snowboarding, snowmobiling, or just taking a lift to view the mountain range and lovely scenery. Oftentimes, the scenery on the ride up to the resort is worth the trip alone. Although this excursion can require more planning than normal, it is well worth it.

Before you plan your snow date, you'll need to check the weather. Verify that your vehicle and its tires are in tip-top shape and pack some tire chains in advance. Research and pay for all the tickets and passes for every activity you two want to participate in. If both of you have never skied or snowboarded before, invest in lessons for a day. If one of you is experienced and the other is not, then it would certainly be worth it for the experienced one to teach the inexperienced some lessons for part of the day. This allows the experienced partner to get in at least a few runs before having to exhibit loving patience with the tumbles and falls that are to follow.

If neither of you want to ski and would rather just enjoy the scenery, I would suggest that you book a cabin with the best scenic views of the area. Being able to sit in the comfort and coziness of your cabin while enjoying a tea ritual is a recipe for love. You might enjoy the added excitement a cabin that offers a big bay window in the bathroom that offers both privacy from others and a beautiful scenic view, so that you and your baby can enjoy a bathing ritual as the sun goes down. If cabins aren't your thing, then you can rent a cottage in a resort area, where you can sit bundled up together on the porch and take in your morning coffee while watching rabbits scamper and deer run across the snow. Don't let the cold weather deter you and your love—snow offers the perfect backdrop for a romantic getaway. It invites opportunities for a variety of the previously discussed rituals and encourages you to cozy up with another, cuddle, hug, embrace, lie closely, and keep each other safe and warm.

Snowed Out Checklist:
- Take proper clothing.
- Check the weather forecast beforehand.
- Prepare your automobile properly.
- Be prepared for a roadside emergency and/or traffic delay.
- Stay on approved roads and courses.
- Be careful and prudent.
- Be freaky and frisky!

Planning Notes:

Who can provide "expert" knowledge, if necessary?

_____

_____

What items do you need to bring?

_____

_____

Where will the activity take place?

_____

_____

When will the activity take place?

_____

_____

Additional Pre-activity Notes:

_____

_____

Post-Activity Notes, Ideas, & Suggestions:

_____

_____

_____

_____

_____

_____

_____

_____

_____

_____

_____

_____

_____

Activity No. 69: A Spiritual High

The last and final destination that will help keep your mutual love alive is taking a spiritual break with your bae. A good spiritual experience can help you both recalibrate, and a spiritual overhauling might be what the two of you need to get your relationship back on track. Go ahead and find a church, synagogue, temple, or YouTube sermon, and with an open heart and mind, expect to have an experience. You two can spend a day listening to sermons that relate to issues in your lives, and perhaps they'll provide the answers that you need.

Another way to tune into the spiritual is to spend the day listening to inspirational, Christian, and/or gospel music. Take a timeout on some hard-to-shake habits that you've been trying to shed, like the use of profanity; intolerant or impatient behaviors; consumption of alcohol, tobacco, and/or marijuana; and the desire to gamble, overeat, or overspend. You can also choose to refrain from activities and objects that you both seem to have little or no control over: this could be your cell phones, scrolling through social media, surfing the net, excessive gaming, etc. Just a single day of restraint and spiritual focus can make a big difference!

Planning Notes:

Who can provide "expert" knowledge, if necessary?

_____

_____

What items do you need to bring?

_____

_____

Where will the activity take place?

_____

_____

When will the activity take place?

_____

_____

Additional Pre-activity Notes:

_____

_____

Post-Activity Notes, Ideas, & Suggestions:

_____

_____

_____

_____

_____

_____

_____

_____

_____

_____

_____

_____

Translations

Pg. 9: I'd like to kiss you by the light of the moon. (Italian)

Pg. 17: I love you with all my heart. (Korean)

Pg. 36: There is nothing that can overpower a man like a woman. (Swahili)

Pg. 54: Together with you is my favorite place to be. (Arabic)

Pg. 61: I love you just the way you are. (Spanish)

Pg. 89: I'm head over heels in love with you. (German)

Pg. 99: I can't stop thinking of you. (Portugese)

Pg. 118: I don't need dreams because I have you. (Japanese)

Pg. 150: I love you forever. (French)

Pg. 166: You are the love of my life. (Punjabi)

Pg. 183: "Your two breasts are like two fawns that are twins of a gazelle." Song of Songs 7:4 (Hebrew)

Pg. 218: In the eyes of her lover, a woman looks like a legendary beauty. (Chinese Mandarin)

www.ingramcontent.com/pod-product-compliance
Lightning Source LLC
Chambersburg PA
CBHW060447280326
41933CB00014B/2693

9 781735 203010